University Lehigh

The Lehigh Quarterly

Vol. 01

University Lehigh

The Lehigh Quarterly
Vol. 01

ISBN/EAN: 9783337712419

Printed in Europe, USA, Canada, Australia, Japan

Cover: Foto ©Andreas Hilbeck / pixelio.de

More available books at **www.hansebooks.com**

Preparatory ✳ School

FOR

LEHIGH UNIVERSITY.

- -

REFERENCES:

R. A. Lamberton, LL.D., President of Lehigh University, and the Professors comprising the Faculty of Lehigh University.

———

Fifty-two of our scholars have been admitted to the present Freshman Class and 368 of them have been admitted to the University since 1880.

Attention is given exclusively to the requirements for admission to Lehigh University.

The Mathematics are in charge of A. E. Meaker, C.E., senior instructor of Mathematics in Lehigh University.

The Physics is in charge of H. S. Houskeeper, B.A., senior instructor of Physics in Lehigh University.

The other instructors are graduates of the University.

Our work is our reference. This work alone has secured the unanimous endorsement of the University Faculty.

Twenty scholars are admitted as boarders to the house of the Principal.

For catalogues and particulars apply to

WM. ULRICH, PRINCIPAL,

26 New Street, Bethlehem, Pa.

HENRY S. JACOBY, C.E.

THE

LEHIGH QUARTERLY.

FOUNDED BY THE CLASS OF 1891.

EDITORS:

GEO. S. HAYES, OHIO.

FRED. C. E. LAUDERBURN, PA.   PAUL M. PAINE, PA.

BUSINESS MANAGERS:

H. K. LANDIS, PA.   H. H. DAVIS, PA.

Vol. I.   JANUARY, 1891.   No. 1.

LEHIGH UNIVERSITY PRECISE TRIANGULATION.

BY HENRY S. JACOBY, C.E., ASSISTANT PROFESSOR OF CIVIL ENGINEERING, CORNELL UNIVERSITY.

The object of this article is to give the results of the final reduction of the precise triangulation at Lehigh University, together with a brief outline of the methods employed both in the field work and the subsequent computations. It may be well, however, to introduce the subject by a short history of the work.

FIELD WORK.

The measurement of the angles and base lines was begun in 1886 and completed in 1889. With a few exceptions, to be indicated hereafter, all of the work was done by members of the Senior Class in the department of Civil Engineering in the course of their regular practice in higher surveying, and under the direction of Professor Mansfield Merriman.

Three monuments were established in April, 1886, named H, K, and L. Near the Sayre Observatory a monument had been previously placed for use in azimuth observations and was known as Station A, or the "azimuth stone." During the season of 1886 the distance from H to K was measured as a base line by means of a standard steel tape. The stations H, K, and L were occupied and the angles measured between them, engineers' transits being used. These stations were also connected with the spires of the Reformed Church in Bethlehem and of Packer Hall on the University campus, by observing directions to them from H and L. The geodetic coördinates of these spires, designated by R and P respectively, had been determined in the preceding year by Professor Merriman for the U. S. Coast and Geodetic Survey.

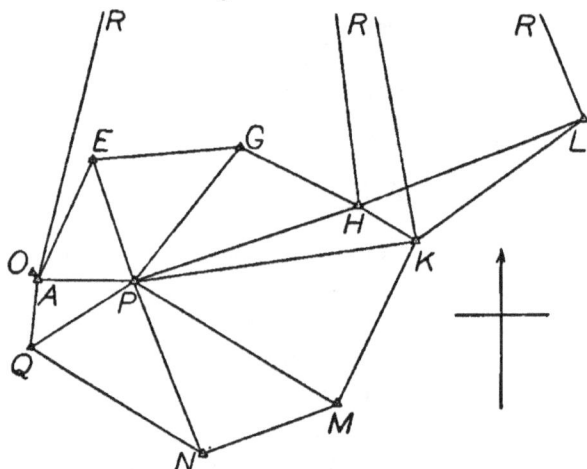

In 1887 three additional permanent stations, G, M, and N, were established and also a temporary one, F, referred to point E, 7.3 feet distant on the curb line, as it did not appear as if A were visible from any point on the curb in that vicinity. Later, when some of the leaves had fallen from the trees, it was found that A and E were intervisible. The distance from F to G was measured as a base line and the distance E G computed from it. This base was more than double the length of H K. Angles were measured at F, G, and A, the last named station being connected with O, the center of the dome of the Sayre Observatory, by means of a small triangle, one of whose sides was measured as a base. A few angles were observed at M and N, but not enough to locate them.

In the spring of 1888 Mr. S. W. Frescoln measured the angles at the permanent station E and re-measured some of those at A, G, and H as a part of his thesis work. In the fall of the same year the base line E G was measured by the Seniors, and the last new station (Q) established and referenced, but only as a temporary one. Only one angle was measured at Q, but all the other stations were again occupied except E and G.

In 1889 the base line E G was measured several times and the polygon around Packer Hall spire as a central station completed by observing the angles at Q. All stations of the system that could be occupied were so used and additional observations made of most of the angles, thus completing the field work.

PRELIMINARY REDUCTIONS.

In 1886 a preliminary reduction of triangulation, including stations P, H, K, L, and R, was made by Professor Merriman, the azimuth of 1880 at A having been transferred to the system by angles observed at two temporary stations, F' and G', near the President's residence. After the field work of 1887 another series of computations was made for the single series of triangles from A to L, the same azimuth being used as before. The azimuth from K to R was then computed and its value compared with one observed at K during the same season.

In 1888 Mr. Frescoln, taking this subject for a thesis, adjusted the triangulation and computed the geographical coördinates; first by means of the system of rectangular spheroidal coördinates as explained in the Report of the New York State Survey for 1887, appendix F, and then by using the regular L M Z formulas. In each case the azimuth of 1887 at K was used, and then computed for the bases of 1886 and 1887, the mean of the results being taken. The maximum difference between the latitudes derived by both methods was $0''.001$ and between the longitudes $0''.003$. After this work was completed Professor C. L. Doolittle made another observation for azimuth at A on May 5th, and Mr. Frescoln then re-computed the spheroidal coördinates, and by reducing the differences between them and the first set to seconds of arc the latitudes and longitudes were corrected. He then compared the geodetic and astronomic latitudes and longitudes and found the deflection of the plumb-line in the planes of the meridian and of the prime vertical. The results were given in an article by him in *The Journal of the Engineering Society*, vol. iii, p. 82 (June, 1888).

The last reduction of the triangulation, the results of which are given in this article, was made by the writer in August, 1890, while an instructor in Lehigh University, having superintended the field work during the fall of 1889. The observations made during the four seasons and used in these computations will now be given, preceded by a description of the stations inserted here for convenient reference.

DESCRIPTION OF STATIONS.

Station *A.*—A small hole in the top of a square stone monument set nearly level with the surface of the ground about 45 feet S 5° E from the south-east corner of the Sayre Astronomical Observatory.

Station *E.*—The centre of a hole drilled in the curbstone about 55 feet east of the north-east corner of Vine Street and Packer Avenue, South Bethlehem. The centre is marked by a small screw in a wooden plug driven into the hole.

Station *F.*—A screw placed in a stout stake. If the line from *G* to *F* is produced 7.458 feet, and that point marked *f*, *E* is 1.967 feet distant from *f*, 7.302 feet from *F*, and situated south of the line *f F*.

Station *G.*—The centre of a hole (marked in the same manner as *E*,) in the curb on the north side of Packer Avenue about 50 feet from the north-west corner of this avenue with Elm Street. It is nearly south from the east side of the gate in front of the south door of the Moravian Church.

Station *H.*—A small hole in centre of square (8″ x 8″) monument 49 feet south of the fence on south side of Lehigh University athletic grounds; also about 60 yards S. 73° E. of south-west corner of athletic grounds, and about 80 yards S. 65° E. of south-west corner of grand stand of athletic grounds.

Station *K.*—A stone monument like *H* situated about 70 yds. N. 31° E. from the north-east corner of the Saucon brick school-house; also about 110 yards S. 18° W. from the south-east corner athletic grounds. It is very nearly in range with the Bethlehem Reformed Church spire and the eastern goal on the athletic grounds.

Station *L.*—A small hole in centre of square (8″x8″) monument about 75 yds. S. from centre of Fifth Street; also about 140 yds. S. 65° W. of north-west corner of house on south-east corner of Fifth and Oak Streets, and about 110 yds. S. 46° E. of north-east corner of house on south-west corner of Fifth and Poplar Streets, also bearing S. 62° W. of north-west corner of public school house near St. Michael's Cemetery.

Station *M.*—The centre of a hole drilled in a rock on the surface of the ground on the north side of South Mountain, about

485 yds. S. 53° E. of Packer Hall spire. It is in range with the small spire of Packer Memorial Church and the southern corner of the Pacific House near the Union Depot; also in the range of the ridge of the Catholic Church in South Bethlehem. It is 6 ft. south-west of the centre of a heap of stones and 6 ft. north-east from a letter M cut on a low flat rock.

Station N.—A hole drilled in the top of a rock with the letter N cut on its side. It is situated about 370 yds. S. $15\frac{1}{4}$° E. of the spire of Packer Hall, and in range with the spires of the Moravian Church in South Bethlehem, and the Salem Lutheran Church in Bethlehem. It is also in range with the spire of Packer Memorial Church and the south-west corner of the Moravian Day-School Hall. It is 10 ft. north-west of the middle of a heap of stones, and 38 ft. south-west of the middle of a wood road.

Station O.—The centre of the dome of Sayre Astronomical Observatory.

Station P.—The spire of Packer Hall, Lehigh University park.

Station Q.—The centre of a small nail in the top of a stout plug driven even with the surface of the ground, about 19 yds. north-east of the south-west corner of University park. It is referenced as follows to two points X and Y. Angle $Q X Y=26°$ 28′ and distance $X Q=11.55$ feet. Angle $Q Y X=10°$ 07′ and distance $Y Q=29.4$ ft. X is a small hole drilled in the top of a rock about 10 yds. from the south fence and 20 yds. from the west fence of University park. Y is a hole in the top of a rock about 6 yds. from the west fence and 20 yds. from the south fence of the park.

Station R.—The spire of the Christ Reformed Church in Bethlehem, Pa.

MEASUREMENT OF ANGLES.

The angles were measured with engineer's transits, the following instruments being used together with the number of angles observed with each one:

Würdemann,	27	Queen,	10
Buff & Berger,	19	Brandis,	14
Fauth,	4	Young,	3
Heller & Brightly,	8		

The Würdemann and Brandis transits read to 20″, the Fauth to 30″ and the rest to single minutes, half of these values being estimated when desired; but this was not often done. The diameters of limb were 5 to 6 inches.

The method of repetitions was employed in observing the angles. As an illustration let the angle PAQ be taken, P being on the left of Q for the observer at A. After clamping the vernier and recording the reading of both verniers, the instrument with telescope direct is set on P by the lower movement, then unclamping the vernier the telescope is pointed on Q by means of the upper movement; the angle has now been measured once and the reading is noted; without changing the reading, the instrument is set again on P by the lower movement, and a second time on Q by the upper movement. The angle has now been measured twice and this is repeated until it is measured four times, when the reading of both verniers is recorded. Had the angle not been noted after being measured once, it would have been necessary to observe the passing of the 360° mark by the zero of the vernier. One set (consisting of four repetitions) has now been completed, and without changing the last reading another set is begun by reversing the telescope and moving in the opposite direction; that is, setting first on Q, then on P, and so on. The third set is begun by shifting to a different part of the circle, the amount of shift depending on the number of readings to be taken, about 90° for 8 sets, or 60° for 12 sets. As many sets with a forward motion should be observed as with a backward motion, but this rule was not always followed, nor that regarding shift, as sometimes the intended work was not completed by the student during the time allotted.

The field notes included the following items: Station occupied, stations observed, time, telescope direct or reversed, number of repetitions, reading of limb, vernier A, vernier B, mean of verniers, difference (between reading at beginning and end of each set of repetitions), angle, observer, and remarks including place, date, instrument used, condition of the atmosphere, and such other items as ought to be known in judging the value of the result, such as interference by smoke from buildings along the line of sight, or the sun being near the line of sight toward evening and when the line of sight is considerably elevated. The following is a copy of the report made for the above angle:

		v	v^2
Angle PAQ	95° 23′ 52″.0	15.75	248.06
48 repetitions.	52.0	15.75	248.06
———	30.0	6.25	39.06
	37.0	0.75	0.56
October 30, 1888,	24.0	12.25	150.06
Fauth transit,	30.0	6.25	39.06
Clear and windy.	48.8	12.55	157.50
	30.0	6.25	39.06
DEANS, ⎱ Observers.	32.5	3.75	14.06
CHESTER, ⎰	31.2	5.05	25.50
	22.5	13.75	189.06
	45.0	8.75	76.56

Mean   95° 23′ 36.25 ± 2.06″   1226.60

$$r = 0.6745 \sqrt{\frac{\Sigma v^2}{n-1}} = 0.6745 \sqrt{\frac{1226.60}{12-1}} = 7''.11,$$

$$r_0 = \frac{r}{\sqrt{n}} = \frac{7.11}{\sqrt{12}} = 2''.06,$$

v being the residuals, Σv^2 the sum of their squares, n the number of observations, r the probable error of a single observation, and r_0 the probable error of the arithmetical mean.

The following is a complete abstract of the angles measured:

ABSTRACT OF ANGLES.

Station occupied.	Angle.	DATE.	No. of repetitions.	VALUE.	Probable error.	Transit.	OBSERVERS.
A	EAP	1888, April 16.	48	65° 49′ 43″.0	1″.74	W	Frescoln.
	PAQ	1888, Oct. 30.	48	95 23 36 .3	2 .06	F	Chester, Deans.
		1889, Oct. 11.	16	40 .3	1 .11	Y	Turner, Nauman.
	EAQ	1889, Oct. 8.	32	161 13 18 .0	2 .18	Br.	Turner, Fleck.
		" " 15.	40	20 .2	2 .68	"	Turner, Nauman.
		" " 18.	48	46 .2	1 .80	BB	Detwiler, Barrett.
	RAE	1888, April 16.	48	11 39 20 .7	1 .76	W	Frescoln.
	RAP	1888, April 17.	48	77 29 04 .7	0 .86	W	Frescoln.
	RAQ	1888, Oct. 16.	32	172 52 42 .0	0 .99	F	Throop, Villalon.
		" " 17.	32	11 .9	1 .65	"	Deans, Wright.
E	GEA	1888, April 12.	48	121 01 14 .9	1 .47	W	Frescoln.
		1889, Oct. 17.	32	27 .2	2 .53	W	Fisher, DeMoyer.
	GEP	1888, April 13.	48	75 43 23 .3	2 .35	W	Frescoln.
		1889, Nov. 1.	32	19 .5	2 .4	BB	Potter, Fisher.
	PEA	1888, April 13.	48	45 17 42 .6	2 .17	W	Frescoln.

ABSTRACT OF ANGLES.—Continued.

Station occupied	Angle	DATE	No. of repetitions	VALUE	Probable error	Transit	OBSERVERS
G	HGE	1888, April 8.	48	148° 50' 22".6	1".19	W	Frescoln.
		1889, Oct. 8.	32	07 .5	2 .13	W	Fisher, DeMoyer.
		" " 15.	48	18 .1	1 .88	BB	Kulp, Detwiler.
	HGP	1888, April 8.	48	103 41 08 .8	1 .76	W	Frescoln.
		1889, Oct. 25.	24	40 26 .0	6 .6	HB	Nauman, Riddick.
	PGE	1888, April 17.	48	45 09 20 .0	1 .09	W	Frescoln.
H	RHL	1886, Oct. 7.	28	76 32 55 .9	2 .39	W	Meily.
	..	1889, Oct. 11.	48	45 .0	2 .31	BB	Kulp, Detwiler.
		" " 18.	32	33 07 .0	2 .03	Y	Nauman, Hoover.
	LHK	1886, Oct. 10.	28	50 41 52 .1	2 .02	W	Reissler.
	KHP	1886, Oct. 21.	32	131 13 47 .9	2 .79	W	Snyder.
		1888, Sept. 19.	48	54 .3	1 .44	BB	Throop, Wright.
		1889, Oct. 24.	40	14 02 .2	0 .57	BB	Sherman, Fisher.
	PHG	1887,Oct.12,21	48	44 06 44 .9	——	W	Domenech, Marshall,
		1888, April 9.	24	07 05 .0	1 .56	W	Frescoln. [Frescoln.
		" Sept. 18.	24	07 07 .5	1 .84	Q	Taylor, Throop.
	GHR	1888, April 8.	48	57 23 58 .7	1 .51	W	Frescoln.
		1889, Oct. 3.	28	24 15 .2	2 .06	Br.	Beazell, Boyd.
	PHR	1886,Oct.15,18	48	101 31 08 .6	0 .94	W	Reissler, Bonnot.
K	HKL	1886, Oct. 6.	32	114 48 50 .6	1 .02	W	Reissler.
	LKM	1889, Oct. 18.	32	150 41 02 .4	3 .42	Br.	Perkins, VanCleve.
	MKP	1887, Oct 6, 7.	48	55 52 32 .9	3 .0	W	Domenech.
		1888, Sept. 18.	40	32 .3	1 .02	BB	Henderson, Diebitsch.
		1889, Oct. 3, 4.	104	23 .9	1 .3	BB	Cardenas, Fink.
	PKH	1886, Oct. 6.	32	38 37 28 .4	1 .74	W	Pratt.
	LKP	1886, Oct. 7.	28	206 33 24 .5	1 .47	W	Reissler.
	PKR	1888, Sept. 26.	24	87 52 43 .8	2 .	Q	Hudson, Cornelius.
		" Oct. 10.	48	47 .3	1 .15	BB	Cornelius, Stockett.
		" " 16.	32	56 .2	0 .86	Q	Lincoln, Gaston.
	RKL	1889, Oct. 17.	48	65 33 39 .4	3 .64	HB	Straub, VanCleve.
	MKR	1888, Oct. 9.	32	143 45 14 .0	1 .97	BB	Diebitsch, Chester.
		" " 16.	32	44 53 .6	1 .5	Q	Lincoln, Gaston.
L	KLR	1886, Oct. —.	56	100 58 15 .3	2 .24	W	Reissler, Pratt, Snyder.
		1888, Sept. 25.	48	44 .3	2 .32	—	Wright, Taylor.
	KLH	1886, Oct. 13.	40	14 28 57 .9	1 .98	W	Reissler, Meily.
		1889, Oct. 25.	56	29 00 .0	0 .92	BB	F. E. and F. R. Fisher.
	HLR	1886, Oct. 12.	36	86 29 09 .9	2 .09	W	Pratt, Reissler.
		1889, Oct. 15.	28	22 .6	4 .34	Y	Perkins, Phillips.
M	NMK	1888, Sept. 25.	48	135 50 24 .0	2 .54	BB	Stockett, Lincoln.
		1889, Oct. 24.	36	51 20 .0	1 .12	W	Barrett, Detwiler.
		" Nov. 5.	32	51 04 .7	1 .6	BB	Riddick, Kulp.

ABSTRACT OF ANGLES.—Continued.

Station occupied	Angle.	DATE.	No. of repetitions	VALUE.	Probable error.	Transit.	OBSERVERS.
M	NMP	1888, Oct. 2.	64	49° 13′ 37″.0	1″.64	Q	Diebitsch, Villalon.
	"	Oct. 3.	48	44 .0 1	.07	BB	Diebitsch, Gaston.
		1889, Oct. 17.	56	17 .4 2	.27	BB	Kulp, Detwiler.
	PMK	1888, Sept. 19.	16	86 37 41 .9 4	.45	HB	Gaston, Villalon.
	"	Sept. 25.	48	08 .2 1	.41	BB	Stockett, Lincoln.
	"	Oct. 2.	32	19 .0 3	.14	Q	Villalon, Diebitch.
		1889, Oct. 25.	24	27 .5 3	.97	HB	Sherman, Kurtz.
N	QNM	1888, Oct. 16.	16	129 56 05 .9 2	.19	BB	Oberly, Wright.
	"	Oct. 17.	16	23 .6 6	.15	Q	Oberly, Barnard.
		1889, Oct. 3.	32	55 52 .3 3	.8	HB	Fleck, Goodman.
	"	Oct. 15.	24	56 11 .7 8	.6	HB	Straub, VanCleve.
	QNP	1888, Oct. 9.	32	36 34 52 .1 2	.6	Q	Throop, Wright.
	"	Oct. 17.	16	52 .5 2	.77	Q	Barnard, Oberly,
		1889, Oct. 8.	44	54 .9 4	.21	HB	Shoemaker, Baily.
	PNM	1887, Oct. 12.	48	93 21 16 .3 0	.99	BB	Focht.
		1888, Sept. 18.	24	46 .5 4	.28	W	Lincoln, Hudson.
	"	Sept. 26.	64	35 .3 1	.89	Q	Lincoln, Henderson.
	"	Oct. 2.	48	09 .6 2	.54	BB	Henderson, Gaston,
Q	AQN	1888, Oct. 10.	56	113 16 46 .9 0	.83	F	Throop, Merriman.
		1889, Oct. 17.	32	52 .0 4	.35	Br.	Perkins, Phillips.
	"	Nov. 14.	44	17 07 .0 2	.14	Br.	{ DeMoyer, Kulp, Perkins, Fisher.
	AQP	1889, Oct. 25.	24	52 04 26 .0 0	.6	Br.	Kulp, Baily.
	"	Oct. 29.	44	59 .4 3	.6	"	Kurtz, Neumeyer.
	"	Nov. 5.	32	42 .5 1	.9	"	{ VanCleve, Phillips, F. E. & F. R. Fisher.
	"	Nov. 19.	32	28 .1 1	.5	"	Howe, Neumoyer.
	"	Nov. 7.	20	25 .5 1	.86	"	Riddick, Howe.
	PQN	1889, Nov. 1.	64	61 12 04 .2 1	.45	Br.	Neumeyer, Riddick.
	"	Nov. 5.	32	21 .7 1	.21	"	Sherman, Perkins.
	"	Oct. 24.	32	11 56 .3 1	.2	"	VanCleve, Shoemaker.

In these 85 measurements of the angles the number of repetitions varies, with one exception, from 16 to 64, the average being 40. The average probable error is 2″.23, the minimum 0″.83 and the maximum 8″.60, only three being above 4″.45.

The following angles were rejected for the reasons indicated. $K L R$, 1889, Oct. 24, 100° 58′ 16″.9, $r_9 = 11″.30$. Original notes show that at the completion of each alternate set of readings the vernier read several minutes more or less than at the beginning of the preceding sets. The notes also stated that the sun was in the direction of K and made it difficult to see the signal.

$N M K$, 1889, Nov. 1, 135° 50' 16''.4, r_0=10''.3. The remarks in the field notes state that the signal at N was scarcely distinguishable, as the sun was in the line of sight.

$Q N M$, 1889, Oct. 4, 129° 58' 16''.6, r_0=11''.3. Signal at Q very indistinct, hazy, and very high wind.

Two or three others were rejected, as the original notes were incomplete or plainly indicated a lack of care in making the observations.

From the small triangle connecting A and O the distance between these two points was found to be 51.802 feet, and the angle $O A R$ was 48° 26'.

SIGNALS.

The form of signals used was of a simple but ingenious type devised by Professor Merriman. It consisted of a wooden tripod, a little smaller than that of an ordinary transit, through the head of which a hole was bored to admit a flag-pole made of gas-pipe about half an inch in diameter. The pole was provided with a point of steel. By means of a plumb-bob the tripod was set up so that the hole in the top was directly above the station, and in this position would hold the pole truly vertical. The pole was painted in the usual manner, lengths of one foot each being alternately red and white. These signals answered their purpose admirably, being light in weight, quickly set up and removed, and subtend a very small angle, which at short sights may be readily bisected.

ELEVATIONS OF STATIONS.

The following elevations of the triangulation stations are given in feet and referred to mean sea level, and as no line of precise levels over these stations has been completed the values are given only to the nearest tenth of a foot. They are the means of a number of determinations made by the Sophomore and Junior Civil Engineering students in their practice with the level.

STATION.	ELEVATION.	STATION.	ELEVATION.
A	363.9	L	302.8
E	315.3	M	594.5
G	298.9	N	628.8
H	337.3	P	577.4
K	376.2	Q	440.7

MEASUREMENT OF THE BASE LINES.

The base lines were measured by means of a standard steel tape 400 feet long, manufactured by Heller & Brightly about 1883. Each base line was divided into as many parts as were needed to make each one shorter than the tape, stout plugs being set at these points of division and each point marked by the notch in the head of a small screw placed in the top of the plug. The elevations of these plugs were carefully determined, as well as those of monuments or stations marking the extremities of the line. Each of these main divisions was subdivided into equal parts by light stakes set in line and on the grade between the end plugs, the distance between these stakes being about fifty feet or less. Two nails were placed on the top of the stakes to keep the tape in position. When these preliminaries were arranged for the entire line the actual measurement was begun by suspending the tape over the plugs and stakes as supports, these being high enough for the tape to clear the ground between the stakes when under tension. A spring balance was attached to the tape at each end of the division to be measured, the pull on the same being recorded. The tape was so held by the balances that at one end a ten-foot mark coincided with the mark on the plug, and at the other end the distance from the nearest foot mark to the mark on the plug was measured by a separate scale to the nearest thousandths of a foot. The temperature of the atmosphere was also taken at the same time and recorded. Six measurements were generally made in succession, two with a pull of 16, 18, and 20 pounds respectively.

BASE LINE H K.

Date.	Divisions.	No. of subdivisions.	Diff. in elevation of ends.	Temperature.	Pull.	Reading.
			feet.		lbs.	feet.
Oct. 13, 1886.	K M	4	16.57	72°	16	191.600
				70	18	191.592
	M H	4	22.41	70	16	220.251
				70	18	220.243

BASE LINE *H K.*—Continued.

Date.	Divisions.	No. of sub-divisions.	Diff. in elevation of ends.	Temperature.	Pull.	Reading.
			feet.		lbs.	feet.
Oct. 20, 1886.	H N	7	38.04	65	16	382.782
				65	18	382.771
				62	16	382.798
				62	18	382.787
				61	16	382.799
				61	18	382.789
	N K	1	0.94	61	16	29.109
				60	16	29.110
Oct. 22, 1886.	K P	2*	7.908	68	16	96.530
				68	20	96.524
				67	16	96.525
				67	20	96.520
	P H	6	31.072	67	16	315.331
				67	20	315.312
				68	16	315.334
				68	20	315.315
Oct. 22, 1886.	K R	2*	7.908	69	16	96.569
				69	20	96.565
				71	16	96.569
				71	20	96.562
	R H	6	31.072	68	16	315.280
				68	20	315.261
				70	16	315.290
				70	20	315.263

*Only one is to be corrected for sag.

BASE LINE *F G*

Date.	Division.	No. of sub-divisions.	Diff. in elevation of ends.	Temperature.	Pull.	Reading.	Remarks.
			feet.		lbs.	feet.	
Oct. 14, 1887.	F F'	1	0.061	55°	16	11.380	
				55	16	11.380	
				54	18	11.380	Cloudy, high winds.
				54	18	11.380	
				54	20	11.380	
				54	20	11.380	
Oct. 7, 1887.	F' X	8	4.585	82	16	399.028	
				81	16	399.034	
				80	18	399.015	Mostly clear, no wind.
				79	18	399.019	
				79	20	398.997	
				79	20	398.999	

BASE LINE *F G.*—Continued.

Date.	Divisions.	No. of subdivisions.	Diff.in elevation of ends.	Temperature.	Pull.	Reading.	Remarks.
			feet.		lbs.	feet.	
Oct. 12, 1887.	F′X	8	4.585	52	16	399.114	
				52	16	399.112	
				51½	18	399.094	Cloudy, wind brisk.
				51	18	399.095	
				51	20	399.081	
				51	20	399.079	
Oct. 14, 1887.	X Y	5	4.622	56	16	216.962	
				57	16	216.956	
				56	18	216.951	Cloudy, high wind.
				57	18	216.943	
				57	20	216.940	
				56	20	216.940	
Oct. 14, 1887.	Y G	7	7.308	56	16	287.925	
				55¾	16	287.924	
				56	18	287.915	Cloudy, high wind.
				56	18	287.914	
				56	20	287.904	
				56	20	287.905	
Oct. 21, 1887.	F F′	1	0.061	61	16	11.381	
				59	18	11.379	Wind brisk.
				58	20	11.379	
Oct. 21, 1887.	F′ S	8	4.551	61	16	399.087	
				61	16	399.087	
				60	18	399.061	Wind brisk.
				61	18	399.061	
				58	20	399.062	
				59	20	399.062	
Oct. 19, 1887.	S W	5	4.824	61.5	16	217.003	
				60.5	16	217.006	
				60.5	18	216.993	Sun and clouds, almost
				61	18	216.993	calm.
				61	20	216.988	
				60	20	216.987	
Oct. 21, 1887.	S W	5	4.574	52	16	217.069	
				52	16	217.073	
				52	18	217.063	Cloudy, windy.
				51.5	18	217.061	
				51.5	20	217.053	
				51.5	20	217.053	
Oct. 19, 1887.	W G	7	7.212	58	16	287.883	
				57	16	287.883	
				56	18	287.870	Cloudy, almost calm
				56	18	287.871	
				56	20	287.861	
				56	20	287.861	

BASE LINE *FG*.—Continued.

Date.	Division.	No. of sub-division.	Diff. in eleva-tion of ends.	Temper-ature.	Pull.	Reading.	Remarks.
			feet.		lbs.	feet.	
Oct. 21, 1887.	W G	7	7.462	52°	16	287.828	
				52	16	287.830	
				52	18	287.820	
				52.5	18	287.818	Cloudy, windy.
				52.5	20	287.807	
				52.5	20	287.809	

BASE LINE *E G*.

Date.	Division.	No. of sub-divisions.	Diff. in eleva-tion of ends.	Temper-ature.	Pull.	Reading.	Remarks.
			feet.		lbs.	feet.	
Oct. 2, 1888.	I	6	7.941	53.5	16	279.891	
				"	18	279.882	Very cloudy, with drops
				"	20	279.871	of rain occasionally.
				"	16	279.891	Rather windy and cold.
				"	18	279.882	
				"	20	279.874	
	II	7	5.624	53.5	16	332.638	
				"	18	332.626	
				"	20	332.610	
				"	16	332.631	
				"	18	332.619	
				"	20	332.610	
	III	7	2.812	53	16	309.904	
				"	18	309.891	
				"	20	309.882	
				"	16	309.902	
				"	18	309.882	
				"	20	309.879	
Oct. 3, 1888,	III	7	2.813	51	16	309.865	Cloudy and windy.
				50.5	18	309.857	
				50.5	20	309.842	
				50	16	309.870	
				50	18	309.857	
				49.5	20	309.845	
	II	7	5.618	48	16	332.736	
				47.5	18	332.727	
				47.5	20	332.712	
				47	16	332.740	
				47	18	332.726	
				47	20	332.715	
	I	6	7.924	47	16	279.850	
				47	18	279.843	
				47	20	279.832	
				48	16	279.848	
				48.5	18	279.840	
				48	20	279.837	

BASE LINE E G.—Continued.

Date.	Divisions.	No. of sub-divisions.	Diff. in eleva-tion of ends.	Tempera-ture.	Pull.	Reading.	Remarks.
			feet.		lbs.	feet.	
Oct. 4, 1889.	G B	6	7.783	64°	16	286.642	Cloudy, sun obscured
4.05 P.M.				"	16	286.642	during entire measure-
				"	18	286.623	ment. Atmosphere
				"	18	286.623	slightly moist.
				"	20	286.612	
				"	20	286.610	
	B A	6	5.280	62	16	265.441	
				"	16	265.441	
				"	18	265.430	
				"	18	265.427	
				"	20	265.413	
				"	20	265.412	
	A E	8	3.338	61.5	16	370.300	
				"	16	370.300	
				"	18	370.277	
				"	18	370.277	
				61	20	370.271	
				"	20	370.270	
Oct. 4, 1889.	B G	6	7.783	56	16	286.638	Cloudy, sun obscured
5.40 P.M.				57	16	286.637	during entire measure-
				57	18	286.617	ment. Atmosphere
				56.5	18	286.620	slightly moist.
				56	20	286.617	
				55.5	20	286.617	
	A B	6	5.280	55	16	265.450	
				"	16	265.450	
				"	18	265.445	
				54.5	18	265.443	
				"	20	265.420	
				"	20	265.420	
	E A	8	3.338	54	16	370.327	
				"	16	370.327	
				53	18	370.297	
				"	18	370.295	
				"	20	370.275	
				54	20	370.275	
Oct. 29, 1889.	X G	4	5.517	48.5	16	198.380	Cloudy and damp.
4.00 P.M.				"	16	198.381	
				"	18	198.372	
				"	18	198.374	
				"	20	198.367	
				"	20	198.366	
	Y X	7	6.699	48	16	324.642	
				"	16	324.640	
				"	18	324.624	
				"	18	324.624	
				"	20	324.606	
				"	20	324.608	

BASE LINE *E G.*—Continued.

Date.		Divisions.	No. of sub-divisions.	Diff. in eleva-tion of ends.	Tempera-ture.	Pull.	Reading.	Remarks.
				feet.		lbs.	feet.	
Oct. 29, 1889.	E Y	9		4.004	48	16	399.441	
4.00 P.M.					"	16	399.441	
					47.5	18	399.423	
					"	18	399.423	
					"	20	399.409	
					"	20	399.409	
Oct. 29, 1889.	G X̄	4		5.517	47	16	198.387	Cloudy, atmosphere
4.35 P.M.					"	16	198.382	damp.
					"	18	198.373	
					"	18	198.372	
					"	20	198.366	
					"	20	198.365	
	X Y	7		6.699	47	16	324.640	
					"	16	324.638	
					46.5	18	324.603	
					46	18	324.603	
					"	20	324.610	
					"	20	324.603	
					"	20	324.603	
	Y E	9		4.004	46	16	399.438	
					"	16	399.440	
					"	18	399.433	
					"	18	399.427	
					"	20	399.433	
					"	20	399.433	

NOTE.—As the brass graduation mark at 280 feet on the tape was lost the tape was held at the nearer edge of the channel in which the mark had been. This affected the measurement of divisions *B G* and *G B* of the base line *E G* on Oct. 4, 1889. The correction to be applied was determined by marking off two points exactly 10 feet apart on a level surface by another ten-foot division of the tape and checking it by three other divisions of the same length. On comparing with this distance the length from the 270-foot mark to the nearer edge of the channel at 280 it was found to be 0.0047 feet too short. This amount 'must therefore be subtracted from the measured distance.

CORRECTIONS AND RESULTS.

The observed distances were corrected for temperature, sag, pull, and grade, by using the following formulas:*

* For the derivation of these formulas see Johnson's Theory and Practice of Surveying, page 457 et seq.

Correction for temperature $= C_t = + \propto (T - T_o)\, L,$

Correction for sag $= C_s = - \dfrac{L}{24}\left(\dfrac{wd}{P}\right)^2,$

Correction for pull $= C_p = + \dfrac{(P - P_o)\, L}{A\,E},$

Correction for grade $= C_g = - \dfrac{h^2}{2L},$ or $- (L - \sqrt{L^2 - h^2}),$

in which $\propto$ = coefficient of expansion of the tape for $1°$ Fahrenheit;

T = observed temperature;

T_o = temperature at which the true length of the tape is the graduated length for the standard pull P_o;

L = observed reading, or length of the tape used in each measurement;

w = weight per linear foot of tape;

d = distance between supports;

P = actual pull on the tape;

P_o = pull at which the tape is standard;

A = area of cross section of tape;

E = coefficient of elasticity of the tape;

h = difference of elevation between the extremities of the uniform grade of each division of the base line.

The steel tape used was stated by the makers to be standard at $56°\,F$, with a tension of 16 pounds, and *no* sag. The constants for the tape were determined by H. Palmer in 1888, as a part of his thesis work. The logarithms of the values obtained are also given here for convenient reference.

CONSTANTS.	VALUES.	LOGARITHMS.
$\propto$	0.00000703	$\overline{6}.8469553$
w	0.0066 pounds.	$\overline{3}.8195439$
A	0.00199 square inches.	3.2988531
E	28,200,000 pounds per sq. inch.	7.4502491
T_o	$56°\,F.$	
P_o	16 pounds.	

The formula for the correction of sag may be more conveniently used when written in the form

$$C_s = -\frac{w^2}{24\,P^2} \cdot \frac{L^3}{n^2},$$

the first part of which is a constant, and n the number of subdivisions, or L divided by d. The first formula for grade was used for the base lines $E\,G$ and $F\,G$ and the second one for $H\,K$, the first formula giving correct results only when h is small compared with L.

As an example of the form used in computing the corrections let the measure of October 3, 1888, of division III, base $E\,G$, be taken.

T	P	Read'g.	C_t	C_s	C_p	C_g	Distance.	Div. III.
51.	16	309.865	—.0109	—.0043	0	—.0128	309.8370	$n=7$.
50.5	18	309.857	—.0120	—.0034	+.0110	—.0128	309.8398	$h=2.813$ ft.
50.5	20	309.842	—.0120	—.0028	+.0221	—.0128	309.8365	
50.	16	309.870	—.0131	—.0043	0	—.0128	309.8398	
50.	18	309.857	—.0131	—.0034	+.0110	—.0128	309.8387	
49.5	20	309.845	—.0142	—.0028	+.0221	—.0128	309.8373	

Mean inclined distance = 309.8510 feet.
Mean horizontal distance = 309.8382 feet.

The value of L used in obtaining the corrections C_t, C_s and C_p was the mean of the readings, and to find C_g the mean inclined distance was taken after the preceding corrections had been applied, in this case 309.8510 feet. After treating each division in this manner, the following reduced horizontal lengths of the base lines were obtained:

BASE LINE.	DATE.	LENGTH IN FEET.
$H\,K$	October 13, 1886,	410.0121
	October 20, 1886,	410.0053
	October 22, 1886,	410.0310
	October 22, 1886,	410.0283

Mean = 410.019

BASE LINE.	DATE.	LENGTH IN FEET.
E G	October 7–21, 1887,	922.2294
	October 2, 1888,	922.2255
	October 3, 1888,	922.2235
	October 4, 1889,	922.2200
	October 4, 1889,	922.1971
	October 29, 1889,	922.2210
	October 29, 1889,	922.2172

$$\text{Mean} = 922.219$$

The first value of *E G* was obtained by reduction from the measurement of *F G*, the corrected length of the latter base being 915.1814 feet.

ANGLE ADJUSTMENT.

Where an angle was measured several times, either on different days or in different years, the observed values are combined into one general mean, the weight of each value being the number of repetitions. The adjustment was then made of the angles at each station of the triangulation occupied by an instrument, the method of least squares being employed.* The weights of the various angles were taken as depending only on the repetitions rather than inversely as the squares of their probable errors. This was done on account of the fact that the angles were observed by different men, with different instruments, and under many different conditions. An exception was made in the case of the angle *H G P*, repeated twenty-four times. As confidence in this value was not established by the report, and also as the probable error was large, the weight was reduced one-half, as this affected the values of the other two angles at the same station less than if either its weight were unchanged or the observation entirely rejected.

ANGLES ADJUSTED AT STATIONS.

E A P	65° 49′ 46″.4	*R A E*	11° 39′ 22″.7
P A Q	95 23 43 .1	*R A Q*	172 52 52 .2
G E P	75 43 26 .0	*R A P*	77 29 09 .1
P E A	45 17 49 .6	*E A Q*	161 13 29 .5
H G P	103 40 59 .1	*G E A*	121 01 15 .6
P G E	45 09 18 .6	*H G E*	148 50 17 .7

* See Merriman's Text Book of Least Squares, Art. 103–105.

ANGLES ADJUSTED AT STATIONS.—*Continued.*

$L H K$	50°	42′	00″.6	$R H L$	76°	32′	56″.5
$K H P$	131	13	57 .2	$G H R$	57	24	06 .1
$P H G$	44	06	59 .6	$P H R$	101	31	05 .7
$K L H$	14	29	03 .2	$H L R$	86	29	21 .7
$M K P$	55	52	25 .8	$K L R$	100	58	24 .9
$P K H$	38	37	33 .1	$R K L$	65	33	42 .6
$H K L$	114	48	55 .4	$L K M$	150	41	05 .7
$N M P$	49	13	31 .9	$L K P$	206	33	31 .5
$P M K$	86	37	18 .6	$P K R$	87	52	45 .9
$Q N P$	36	34	48 .5	$M K R$	143	45	11 .7
$P N M$	93	21	22 .6	$N M K$	135	50	50 .5
$A Q P$	52	04	42 .1	$Q N M$	129	56	11 .1
$P Q N$	61	12	09 .7	$A Q N$	113	16	51 .8

$$1259° \; 59′ \; 51″.1$$

The sum of the eight interior angles of the polygon $A E G H$ $K M N Q A$ is 8″.1 less than the required amount, or 1080°, and the angles of the triangle $H K L$ are also 0″.8 too small in the aggregate.

If the angles of this polygon are adjusted for horizon closure by taking them all of equal weight and the base $H K$ is computed from that of $E G$, its value will be 0.040 feet less than the observed value when using the three triangles lying between them; or 0.045 feet less when passing around the larger segment of the polygon. If the same computation is made with the angles adjusted only at the stations the corresponding differences are 0.028 and 0.033 feet. This is, then, a case of discrepancy between bases, and may be adjusted either by throwing the entire error into the base lines or into the angles, or partly into both. It was decided to leave the base lines unchanged, hence the angles must satisfy the following conditional equations:

$$\frac{HK}{EG} = \frac{\sin GEP}{\sin GPE} \cdot \frac{\sin PGH}{\sin PHG} \cdot \frac{\sin HPK}{\sin HKP},$$

$$\frac{HK}{EG} = \frac{\sin EGP}{\sin EPG} \cdot \frac{\sin PEA}{\sin PAE} \cdot \frac{\sin PAQ}{\sin PQA} \cdot \frac{\sin PQN}{\sin PNQ} \cdot \frac{\sin PNM}{\sin PMN} \cdot$$

$$\frac{\sin PMK}{\sin PKM} \cdot \frac{\sin KPH}{\sin KHP}.$$

$$PHG + GHP + PHK + HKP + PKM + \ldots\ldots + $$
$$PEA + EGP - 1080° = 0.$$

After completing this polygonal adjustment† in which the angles were taken of equal weight, the angles were again adjusted at station H, at station K, for triangle HKL, at station L, and at station A, successively, without disturbing the values previously adjusted, the correction for any angle not exceeding 0″.7. The adjusted angles are here given, these being the final values except for those affected by the position of R, the final values of which will be given later.

EAP	65°	49′	46″.8
PAQ	95	23	43 .9
GEP	75	43	27 .1
PEA	45	17	51 .7
HGP	103	41	00 .0
PGE	45	09	19 .8
KHP	131	13	54 .9
PHG	44	06	59 .9
MKP	55	52	26 .1
PKH	38	37	33 .1
NMP	49	13	32 .0
PMK	86	37	19 .6
QNP	36	34	48 .1
PNM	93	21	.23 .5
AQP	52	04	42 .2
PQN	61	12	11 .3
1080°	00′	00″.0	

*GHR	57°	24′	06″.7
*RHL	76	32	57 .2
LHK	50	42	01 .3
HKL	114	48	55 .3
*HKR	49	15	12 .8
*RKL	65	33	42 .5
KLH	14	29	03 .4
*HLR	86	29	21 .6
*RAE	11	39	22 .1

* See p. 24 for final values.

APE	68°	52′	21″.5
EPG	59	07	13 .1
GPH	32	12	00 .1
HPK	10	08	32 .0
KPM	37	30	14 .3
MPN	37	25	04 .5
NPQ	82	13	00 .6
QPA	32	31	33 .9
360°	00′	00″.0	

† Wright's Adjustment of Observations, page 309 et. seq.

TRIANGLE SIDES, DIRECTION ANGLES, AND PLANE CO-ORDINATES.

Next in order, the sides of all the triangles composing the polygon around P were computed, beginning with the base $E G$ and checking on the base $H K$ and the side $P G$, and also those of the triangle $H K L$. The lengths obtained are given in the table on page 27. Then starting with the azimuth observed at K in 1888 (see page 25) the following direction angles (which are not the final values) were found :

K to R	169°	38′	46″.4		K to P	81°	46′	00″.5
K to L	235	12	28 .9		H to P	71	37	28 .5
H to L	249	41	32 .3		H to R	173	08	35 .1
L to R	156	10	53 .9		P to A	91	25	53 .8
K to H	120	23	33 .6		A to R	193	56	44 .9

From the direction angles and distances the plane coördinates were then computed, those for K being assumed as a starting point.

STATIONS.	LONGITUDE. FEET.	LATITUDE. FEET.
A	4326.412	764.068
H	2353.673	1207.438
K	2000.000	1000.000
L	958.203	1723.851
P	3733.045	749.239

By means of these coördinates the following direction angles and distances were determined:

H to A	77°	20′	00″.0	2021.949 feet.
K to A	84	12	33 .0	2338.345 "
L to A	74	05	41 .7	3502.288 "

and then the triangle sides:

TRIANGLE.	SIDE.	DISTANCE. FEET.
ARH	$\begin{cases} AR \\ HR \end{cases}$	5663.959 5090.046
ARK	$\begin{cases} AR \\ KR \end{cases}$	5664.373 5348.570
ARL	$\begin{cases} AR \\ LR \end{cases}$	5664.378 4960.082
HRK	$\begin{cases} HR \\ KR \end{cases}$	5092.846 5350.988

TRIANGLE.	SIDE.	DISTANCE. FEET.
HRL	$\begin{cases} HR \\ LR \end{cases}$	5090.924 4960.590
KRL	$\begin{cases} KR \\ LR \end{cases}$	5348.579 4960.085

From the direction angles and distances from A, H, K, and L to R the plane coördinates of R were found.

	LONGITUDE. FEET.	LATITUDE. FEET.
From triangle ARH	2961.375	6261.077
ARK	2961.275	6261.479
ARL	2961.275	6261.483
HRK	2961.709	6263.857
HRL	2961.480	6261.948
KRL	2961.276	6261.487
Mean	2961.398	6261.888

This table shows that the intersections of the lines from A, K and L practically coincide, the extreme intersections being only 0.008 feet apart. By plotting these coördinates on a sheet of cross-section paper it was seen that the line from H to R passed westward of the intersection of these three lines and 0.14 feet distant; that is, if the line from H were to be made to pass through this intersection its direction angle would have to be increased a little less than 6″. The intersection of the lines from H and K is 2.41 feet distant (west of north) from the above intersection, the angle between these lines being less than three and a half degrees. Taking all of these facts into consideration and remembering that the work was done by ordinary engineer's transits and a steel tape by four different classes of students in their regular practice extending over very limited periods, the above results may be regarded as very good.

The mean of the above coördinates gives the adjusted position of R, and from these and the plane coördinates of the stations A, H, K and L the revised direction angles and distances are found.

A to R	193°	56′	37″.0	5664.740 feet.
H to R	173	08	38 .1	5090.855 "
K to R	169	38	44 .6	5348.995 "
L to R	156	10	56 .0	4960.523 "

It will be observed that in adjusting the position of R the direction angle from K to R does not now agree with the azimuth at K. The changed direction angles require a corresponding change in all the angles adjacent to them. The following are their new values:

RAE	11°	39′	30″.0	ARH	20°	47′	58″.9
GHR	57	24	09 .7	ARK	24	17	52 .4
RHL	76	32	54 .2	HRK	3	29	53 .5
HKR	49	15	11 .0	KRL	13	27	48 .6
RKL	65	33	44 .3	RAK	70	15	56 .0
HLR	86	29	23 .7	AKR	85	26	11 .6

All the distances are then reduced to meters, their values being given on page 27. One foot equals 0.304797 meters, or the logarithm of any distance in meters equals the logarithm of the distance in feet plus 9.4840111 minus 10.

CONNECTION WITH U. S. C. AND G. S. STATIONS.

Professor Mansfield Merriman, as Acting Assistant of the United States Coast and Geodetic Survey, during the Summer of 1885 occupied six stations, from two of which—Bake Oven and Smith's Gap—he observed directions to the spire of the Reformed Church and that of Packer Hall. The results of these observations and computations are as follows:

BAKE OVEN STATION.—Situated near the boundary line between Carbon and Lehigh Counties about five miles north-west of the village of Germansville:

Latitude, 40° 44′ 54″.109, Longitude, 75° 44′ 02″.222.

To Smith's Gap:	Azimuth,	252°	26′	55″.42;	distance	27535.3 meters,
To Reformed Church:	"	294	52	30 .39	"	33389.8 "
To Packer Hall:	"	297	36	49 .42	"	33932.2 "

SMITH'S GAP STATION.—Situated near the boundary line between Monroe and Northampton Counties, about four miles west of the village of Point Phillips.

Latitude, 40° 49′ 21″.787. Longitude, 75° 25′ 21″.906.

To Bake Oven:	Azimuth,	72°	39′	07″.24;	distance	27535.3 meters
To Reformed Church:	"	349	57	34 .13	"	22710.6 "
To Packer Hall:	"	351	11	08 .84	"	24332.0 "

REFORMED CHURCH SPIRE. — Latitude, 40° 37′ 16″.778. Longitude 75° 22′ 33″.452.

To Bake Oven : Azimuth, 115° 06′ 30″.54; distance 33389·8 meters,
To Smith's Gap : " 169 59 24 .03 " 22710.6 "

PACKER HALL SPIRE. — Latitude, 40° 36′ 22″.257. Longitude, 75° 22′ 43″.318.

To Bake Oven : Azimuth, 117° 50′ 43″.01 ; distance 33932.2 meters.
To Smith's Gap : " 171 12 52 .29 " 24332·0 "

AZIMUTH OBSERVATIONS.

As neither of the stations R and P could be occupied in order to determine the direction to any station of the Lehigh University triangulation from those of the U. S. Coast and Geodetic Survey stations, an azimuth had to be determined astronomically at some station of the former triangulation. The one used in the present reduction is the mean of two azimuths observed by Charles L. Doolittle, the Professor of Mathematics and Astronomy at the University, the one at station A on May 5 and June 7, and the other at station K on May 7 and IJune 5, 1888. A mark was placed at a window on the east side of the frame wing on the east side of the Moravian Day-School Hall, in Bethlehem. The azimuth of this mark from station A was found to be 180° 12′ 58″.4, and from station K was 153° 25′ 54″.9, reckoned from the south point. The angle at A between the mark and R was then measured by a transit, 136 repetitions giving a value of 13° 43′ 38″.6, and the angle between the same points at K was determined by 144 repetitions to be 16° 12′ 51″.5. This gives for the azimuth from A to R 193° 56′ 37″.0; and from K to R 169° 38′ 46″.4.

In order to determine the agreement or the discrepancy between these two observed azimuths it is necessary to compute the angle of convergence of meridians through A, R and K. The angle of convergence of the meridians passing through any two stations is equal to the difference in longitude of the stations reduced to seconds multiplied by the cosine of the mean of their latitudes. For instance, let the stations K and R be taken. The difference in latitude is 961.4 feet, and the mean latitude is approximately 40° 36′ 50″.8. For this latitude each second of longitude equals 23.51 meters,* hence the difference in longitude equals 12″.46 and the angle of convergence 8″.1. The angle of convergence between the meridians through A and R is 11″.5 and of those through A and K is 19″.6.

Observed azimuth K to R,	169°	38′	46″.4
Angle $A R K$,	24	17	52 .4
	193	56	38 .8
Convergence, A and K,			19 .6
Computed azimuth A to R,	193	56	19 .2
Observed azimuth A to R,	193	56	37 .0
Difference,			17″.8

The error of the triangulation combined with the discrepancy between the azimuth observations is therefore 17″.8. Had the line from H to R met the intersection of the lines from A, K, and L, then the above difference would have been reduced 6″.1 or a little more than one-third. As Prof. Doolittle regarded the two azimuths as of equal weight, the following final values are obtained:

Azimuth	A to R,	193°	56′	28″.1
"	R to A,	13	56	39 .6
"	K to R,	169	38	55 .3
"	R to K,	349	38	47 .2

LATITUDES, LONGITUDES, AND AZIMUTHS.

Starting from R with its geodetic coördinates known those of all the other stations were computed with the usual L. M. Z. formulas employed for subordinate triangulation, as given together with the required factors in Appendix No. 7 of the U. S. C. & G. S. Report for 1884.

---

* See U. S. C. & G. S. Report for 1884, page 222 (Appendix No. 6).

Line.	Azimuth.			Distance.	
	°	′	″	feet.	meters.
A to O	145	30	28.1	51.802	15.789
A to R	193	56	28.1	5664.740	1726.598
A to E	205	35	58.1	778.949	237.422
A to P	271	25	44.9	593.552	180.913
A to Q	6	49	28.8	404.567	123.311
E to G	264	34	42.1	922.219	281.090
E to P	340	18	09.2	761.872	232.217
E to A	25	36	00.9	778.949	237.422
G to H	295	44	30.0	797.152	242.970
G to P	39	25	30.0	1041.356	317.403
G to E	84	34	49.8	922.219	281.090
H to R	173	08	45.8	5090.855	1551.679
H to L	249	41	40.0	1487.958	453.526
H to K	300	23	41.3	410.019	124.973
H to P	71	37	36.2	1453.483	443.018
H to G	115	44	36.1	797.152	242.970
K to R	169	38	55.3	5348.995	1630.359
K to L	235	12	39.6	1268.582	386.660
K to M	25	53	45.1	1067.950	325.508
K to P	81	46	11.2	1751.093	533.728
K to H	120	23	44.3	410.019	124.973
L to R	156	11	15.5	4960.523	1511.954
L to K	55	12	48.4	1268.582	386.660
L to H	69	41	51.8	1487.958	453.526
M to N	70	02	49.6	883.839	269.392
M to P	119	16	21.6	1452.087	442.592
M to K	205	53	41.2	1067.950	325.508
N to Q	120	06	31.0	1245.402	379.595
N to P	156	41	19.1	1101.535	335.745
N to M	250	02	42.6	883.839	269.392
Q to A	186	49	28.4	404.567	123.311
Q to P	238	54	10.6	749.092	228.321
Q to N	300	06	21.9	1245.402	379.595
R to A	13	56	39.6	5664.740	1726.598
R to L	336	10	58.6	4960.523	1511.954
R to K	349	38	47.2	5348.995	1630.359
R to H	353	08	40.7	5090.855	1551.679

The latitudes and longitudes of the stations computed from the geodetic coordinates of *R* as determined in 1885, are given in the following table:

STATION.	LATITUDE.			LONGITUDE.		
·A	40°	36′	22″.452	75°	22′	51″.150
E	40	36	29 .393	75	22	46 .786
G	40	36	30 .254	75	22	34 .883
H	40	36	26 .833	75	22	25 .574

STATION.		LATITUDE.			LONGITUDE.	
K	40°	36′	24″.783	75°	22′	20″.989
L	40	36	31 .935	75	22	07 .482
M	40	36	15 .290	75	22	27 .036
N	40	36	12 .310	75	22	37 .806
O	40	36	22 .874	75	22	51 .530
P	40	36	22 .306	75	22	43 .457
Q	40	36	18 .483	75	22	51 .773
R	40	37	16 .778	75	22	33 .452

If the above coördinates be derived from the latitude and longitude of P as determined in 1885 (see page 25) as a standard they would have to be diminished by 0.″049 and 0.″139 respectively. Since Prof. Merriman has assigned the coördinates of R five times the weight of those of P the following final values are obtained by combining the two sets.

FINAL GEODETIC COORDINATES.

STATION.		LATITUDE.			LONGITUDE.	
A	40°	36′	22″.444	75°	22′	51″.127
E	40	36	29 .385	75	22	46 .763
G	40	36	30 .246	75	22	34 .860
H	40	36	26 .825	75	22	25 .551
H	40	36	24 .775	75	22	20 .966
L	40	36	31 .927	75	22	07 .459
M	40	36	15 .282	75	22	27 .013
N	40	36	12 .302	75	22	37 .783
O	40	36	22 .866	75	22	51 .507
P	40	36	22 .298	75	22	43 .434
Q	40	36	18 .475	75	22	51 .750
R	40	37	16 .770	75	22	33 .429

DEFLECTION OF THE PLUMB LINE.

The astronomic latitude of the dome of Sayre Observatory as determined by Prof. Doolittle in 1885–86 is 40° 36′ 23″.512, and the geodetic latitude of 1890 as above is 40° 36′ 22″.866, hence the apparent local deflection of the vertical in the plane of the meridian is $\triangle\phi = A - G = +0″.646$. A + sign indicates the zenith thrown to the north (or plumb line to the south); a — sign the reverse.

The astronomic longitude of the dome of Sayre Observatory as determined by Prof. Doolittle in 1875 is 75° 22′ 58″.545 and the geodetic longitude of 1890 as above is 75° 22′ 51″.507, hence the apparent local deflection of the vertical is $\triangle^\lambda = A - G = +7″.038$; and the apparent local deflection of the vertical in the plane of the prime vertical is $\triangle p = \triangle^\lambda \cos \phi = +5″.343$. In this formula ϕ is the latitude of the observatory. A + sign indicates that the zenith is thrown to the west; a — sign the reverse.

In the astronomic determinations the direction of the plumb line is the vertical, and in the geodetic determinations the normal to the spheroid used (Clarke's) is the vertical at that point.

The above longitudes are all referred to the meridian of Greenwich by using the old longitude of the Naval Observatory of Washington, D. C., (the one in general use) viz: 77° 03′ 01″.35. In Appendix No. 11 of the U. S. Coast and Geodetic Survey Report for 1884 is given the result of the second adjustment by Asst. C. A. Schott of the determinations of the longitude made by means of the electric telegraph between the years 1846 and 1885. This new value is °77 03′ 00″.57 with a probable error of ±0″.62.

These deflections may now be compared with the tabulation and diagrams of the "local deflections of the plumb line at stations of the oblique arc along and near our Atlantic Coast" by Assistant Schott in Appendix No. 8 of the U. S. C. and G. S. Report for 1879.

CONCLUSION.

On examining the results given in this article from measurements made in the manner and by the class of observers indicated, it may be inferred that with careful observations by a surveyor of experience the same class of instruments could be made to have given even better results. By following a systematic programme of angle measurement at each station the time required would be reduced and the adjustment simplified.

It may also be added that with this triangulation as a basis prominent points such as church spires, flagstaffs on public buildings or business houses in the towns of Bethlehem and South Bethlehem may be readily located by taking directions to them from three of the stations, selecting two of them with a view of securing the best angle of intersection on the point to be located, the direction from the third being used as a check. A number of such points carefully determined in various parts of the towns would form an excellent check upon shorter surveys connecting them and made in the usual manner by traversing. A map might thus be produced with ordinary engineer's instruments whose precision would be far in advance of those generally made for towns and cities. By properly selecting the stations so as to obtain a simple system of well proportioned triangles the work required to make a triangulation for this purpose would not be great and the expense incurred would be amply justified when its advantages are taken into account.

CIVIL ENGINEERING.

This article is made up of replies to the following list of questions, which were recently sent to some of our most prominent engineers:

1. What is the present, and probable future demand for civil engineers?

2. What particular branch of civil engineering do you think offers the best inducements to a young engineer?

3. What characteristics in a person tend to show a natural aptitude for civil engineering?

4. What can you say of the attractions which the profession offers to those following it, *i.e.*, mode of life, surroundings, social position?

5. In what way would you advise a young engineer to proceed in obtaining his situation?

Please add all general considerations which may occur to you.

I would say that in a broad sense this profession offers probably as great an inducement to young men as any other department of human activity. To rise to eminence or great success the engineer, like the poet, "must be born, not made." The great bulk of society must be "hewers of wood and drawers of water" under the guidance of a very few whom natural selection has differentiated out of the masses as of superior wisdom and ability. To these few the great prizes are awarded, while the army of followers must be content with such living as they can obtain, shading through various degrees of comfort to a bare existence. To this immutable law the profession of the engineer is no exception.

To be successfully prosecuted, engineering must be recognized as a business as well as a profession, dealing with men and affairs more than with theories. For this reason the best students at college often fail in real life, lacking those qualities which are covered by the phrase "business instinct." On the contrary, mediocre students often make brilliant successes of their lives, through being shrewd judges of human nature and being born with a capacity for generalizing and availing themselves of the the special aptitudes of others. The demands of these days are more exacting than ever before, and a man found wanting is quickly displaced for a new comer who gives promise of capacity and performance. Taking up your questions as you put them, I would say the demand for engineers will last as long as the human race is engaged in enterprises and society is dependent upon avenues of transportation for its well-being ; but where many are contending for place and preferment, only those can expect success who have the engineering instinct, with all the term implies. The possession of a diploma does not make an engineer, nor do purely studential qualities or familiarity with engineering process.

There is no one special branch of engineering which appears to me more promising than another, unless it be marine engineering and shipbuilding, which have barely started in this country. These industries are bound to become important factors in our national development; but their discussion involves economic questions out of place in this letter. Electricity is only promising to those with aptitude for mechanical invention and application, in which its development is taking place. The physics of electricity is simple, and any young man aspiring to be an electrician based upon his familiarity with, and interest in, electricity as a science, will find the field more than occupied. If he has not the mechanical instinct to devise, combine and apply electricity as a servant or a power, he had better let it alone. In the various departments of transportation the training of an engineer is invaluable, and the field of his employment is almost limitless.

It is somewhat difficult to define the characteristics by which a young man should exhibit his aptitude for the engineering profession. There are so many examples of promising young men failing to meet the expectations had for them, and *vice versa.* Many important qualities only develop in after years. Life is more or less of a lottery, and with the average man his success, be it more or less, is a matter of circumstance and opportunity, which some forceful, aggressive characters can evolve for themselves. I should say that any person who finds out that he is not adapted for engineering (which he ought quickly to learn in competition with his fellows) should go at something else. His education is not lost and is valuable in any branch of business or finance.

The attractions of any profession or occupation are as one makes them. The social advantages or disadvantages are matters of purely secondary consideration. A gentleman will always be a gentleman under any circumstances and will make his own position wherever he may be. To the enthusiast in his profession—and enthusiasm belongs to the young—he should crave no other attraction than grows out of his work and the improvement of his opportunities for storing his mind with useful knowledge and actual practice.

As to getting started on his career after graduation, the aspiring engineer must do what any one else must do seeking work, offer himself untiringly until he finds his niche. He should not aim too high, but be willing to start in an humble capacity if only to gain a foothold, trusting by industry, attention to duty and native capacity to prove his worth for advancement. A young man wants to examine himself carefully as to his most natural aptitude, and seek employment in the direction nature has best fitted him; otherwise he will, nine times out of ten, be a failure. He should love his work, throw his whole heart and soul into it, and it will be very unusual if such an one does not win place and position in as grand a profession as man can follow.

ALFRED P. BOLLER.

The present demand for civil engineers is scanty, in consequence of the financial stringency. This will pass away, and in a year or two, new enterprises will afford openings for young men beginning the profession.

The great field hitherto has been in the construction of railroads. This will continue, but to a smaller extent. There will probably be increased opportunities in operating departments of these and similar corporations, as well as in electrical, mechanical and naval engineering, the tendency being to put into the hands of trained scientific men much of the work hitherto done by practical men.

The characteristics which indicate aptitude for civil engineering are mathematical and mechanical tastes and tendencies, together with judicial balance of mind and painstaking accuracy. Sterling integrity is indispensable to success.

The chief attraction which the profession offers is the certainty that, as wealth increases and more expensive enterprises are undertaken, there will be increased demand for trained men to direct them, and a substitution of scientific methods for the cut and try rules of thumb which prevail in new countries with limited capital. In Europe the civil engineers are looked upon as the leaders of modern civilization. They may become such in America, as the rate of interest decreases and profitable investments become more difficult. The mode of life, surroundings and social position will naturally vary with the branch followed and the character of the individual, but no young man should take up the profession with the expectation that it will prove an easy one. Close attention and hard work are necessary to success in this as well as in other pursuits.

The best way for a young engineer to proceed in obtaining his situation is by personal application. He may write letters and enclose testimonials, but they produce little effect in comparison with a five minutes interview, face to face. Inquiries may be made by mail, expressing an intention to apply in person should a vacancy exist or be probable, but as a rule the employing engineer wants to see the "cut of the gib" of the applicant. The next best method is the application or recommendation by an intermediate acquaintance of both parties, who can confidently recommend the young engineer.

As a rule it is best to accept the first engagement which offers, even if the compensation be small. Once the young man is at work, his success is in his own hands, for with close application and willing work he is sure of promotion or recommendation to other employers in want of such services.

O. CHANUTE.

The demand for trustworthy and experienced engineers is always good, provided that the applicant has the qualities usually called for in all business engagements, namely, good manners and address, gentlemanly appearance, etc.

As a large share of the wealth of the country is concentrated in the cities and villages for many years to come it would appear that a demand will exist for engineers skilled in the construction and planning of sewers, water works and street pavements.

Truthfulness, perseverance, habits of exactness, a taste for mathematics and mathematical draughting, are requisites.

It is very rare to find persons in any profession who are thoroughly satisfied with their surroundings, and engineers frequently have cause for dissatisfaction ; still our memory of the unpleasant is apt to be short-lived, while we never forget that which really interests and pleases us. The life of an engineer is not apt to lack variety, and his experiences are apt to be rough ones, yet I think he enjoys his life quite as much as the average man. The engineer is generally a healthy man and uses his faculties to such an extent that he is generally a better developed man than the average, and is open to the heightened sense of enjoyment that is concomitant with such development.

The social position of an engineer is inferior to that of the lawyer or medical man. This arises, as I believe, from the lack of education and culture in many who assume, as they should be prohibited from doing, the title of civil engineer.

He should obtain as good a general and technical education as possible, and should then acquire some experience, even if he has to pay for the privilege. Previous experience is generally quite essential to the procurement of a good situation.

An engineer who intends to devote himself to state or municipal work should thoroughly identify himself with the interests of those with whom and for whom he is to work. In this state (N. Y.) citizenship is a requisite for appointment to engineering positions and non-residents are not generally eligible to appointment in the cities.   HORACE ANDREWS.

The present demand is good, and the future demand will be better.

Railroad engineering. Next to that sanitary and hydraulic engineering.

One who possesses good common sense, with a logical, deliberate and unprejudiced mind, enabling him to arrive at a correct conclusion, as deduced from the real premises; and then with the requisite courage to carry out his convictions.

If a man is really in love with his profession (and unless he is, he will not succeed), he will not regard seriously the hardships of life. His surroundings will be as he will make them, while as for a social position, if he has the proper personal qualifications, he will find his profession aiding him for social advancement. In Europe the engineer is always regarded with the highest esteem.

By taking a course in one of the leading technical schools. The demand to-day is for educated men.

                     WM. BARCLAY PARSONS.

With reference to bridge engineering, capable, reliable and experienced men for engineers and draughtsmen are now in good demand, and will probably be so for a good many years.

Electricity.

An inborn taste for mathematical and drawing studies and a natural, lively interest in the constructive trades and practical mechanics.

The branches of the profession are widely different in nature and location of work, and even in the same branches individual positions vary greatly in surroundings, mode of life and social advantages. The principal attraction in any branch of the profession should be the work itself. If the young engineer feels that he has special talent for a certain line of work, let him, by all means, engage in that work, even with a nominal or no salary. If he has merit his employers will surely discover it and his advancement will follow in good time.   F. C. OSBORN.

THE DEVELOPMENT OF THE COAL AND TIMBER LANDS OF SOUTHEASTERN KENTUCKY.

This article must of necessity be cursory in its nature from the fact that it is scarcely five years since the mineral resources of this region began to attract attention, and it will be our object to deal more with the organization of the land companies, and the methods by which they are securing and surveying their properties, than with the nature and the value of the properties themselves. For a proper understanding of the subject, a partial knowledge of the geographical and meteorological characteristics of the country is required. If a line be drawn across the state from the mouth of the Big Sandy to where the Cumberland crosses into Tennessee nearly all to the east will be found covered by the carboniferous formation. Until we approach the Appalachian system in the south the strata are nearly horizontal, so that, as the coal veins are almost all above the drainage, mines could be drained and operated at a minimum cost. The coal-bearing formation consists mostly of rather hard shale and sandstones, many massive and suitable for building purposes.

The coal measures, all bituminous or cannel, are of immense extent and vary in thickness from a few inches to fourteen feet. Continuous beds may be traced for miles by their outcrop along the streams, varying, of course, in thickness and quality, but nevertheless part of the same ancient forests and jungles that flourished here in bygone ages. The whole is supported by thick conglomerates and is intersected by streams flowing through steep, narrow valleys, which, but for the friability of the rocks, would be cañons. Across the southeastern counties, without a break excepting three water gaps, and for a distance of 150 miles, extends Pine Mountain, a steep, fault ridge, facing to the north and rising perhaps 1000 feet above the neighboring streams. Fifteen or twenty miles farther south is Cumberland Mountain, another fault ridge, but facing in the opposite direction. It is between these two ridges that the finest and deepest coal deposits are found, for the erosion in this confined area has not been as great as to the north. At the base of the faults are exposed the silurian rocks, with their valuable strata of limestone and veins of iron ore, consisting of red hematite, or " red fossiliferous ore," brown hematite and limonite, and also limited but rich manganese deposits, forming altogether an ideal region for the production of iron and steel.

Everywhere the bottoms and some of the hillsides are culti-vated, producing principally corn and a few sweet and white potatoes, so that the stranger, who usually expects to find an unregenerated wilderness, is somewhat disappointed. The climate is moist and rains are frequent, causing a luxuriant vegetation and magnificent timber, chiefly of poplar (tulip tree), beech, oak and walnut. Crops are always successful, but because of the roughness of the soil and the indifference of a miserable and depraved native population there is hardly a respectable farm to be found.

But to return to the subject proper. The first company to enter the field was the American Association (Limited), of Lon-don, England, which acquired 60,000 acres of land in and around Cumberland Gap. They conveyed certain franchises to the Mid-dlesborough Town Company and the result is that in the centre of their admirably selected territory has sprung up a prosperous and growing town of several thousand inhabitants. The follow-ing extract from the opening page of a report of Mr. A. A.

Arthur, trustee of the latter company, will convey an idea of the richness of the surrounding mineral deposits:

The valuable properties of this association, consisting of about 20,000 acres of iron and coal deposits, lie on either side of the Cumberland Gap, where the states of Kentucky, Tennessee and Virginia join their boundary lines. The iron beds are found by themselves on the south side of the Cumberland Mountain, and the coal lands are between the same on its northern slope and the range of the Pine Mountain in Kentucky. The iron ores occupy a long stretch of land lying adjacent to, and running parallel with, the Cumberland Mountains, while the coal measures are above drainage level in the hills, forks, spurs and knobs that fringe the valley of the Big Yellow Creek. The lands containing the ores are partly upon the main mountain, partly in the Poor Valley, partly on the Poor Valley and Powell River ridges, and stretch almost continuously from four or five miles above the gap to about twenty miles below it. The association owns and controls all the mineral lands about the gap, and the right to the ores at other places on option and by contract.

The ores at and near the gap in the section of country above named show by analysis as follows:

	METALLIC IRON.	PHOSPHORUS.	SULPHUR.
Red Fossil Ore . .	58,730	0,041	0.230
Brown Hematite .	56,490	0,006	0.210
Carbonate .	44,660	0.020	traces

	MANGANESE.	IRON.	PHOSPHORUS.
Manganiferous	37,209	5.000	traces

	ZINC.
Zinc	34 per cent.

The red and brown hematite are *good* Bessemer ores.

The carbonate ore is a good foundry ore.

The manganiferous ores will make No. 1 spiegeleisen.

The zinc ore also contains lead, and is said to give $12 per ton of silver.

The hammered bars made from the red ores by charcoal analyze 98.64 per cent. of iron.

The specimens of ores giving the foregoing analyses were taken from the outcrop, and the analyses represent an average of the specimens.

Furnaces are now in construction and it is claimed that the ores can be delivered at a cost for mining and transportation of only $0.65 per ton, while pig iron can be produced at a cost not exceeding $10 per ton. If this estimate be correct, the success of the enterprise is self-evident, and we shall see in Middlesborough, Ky., a rival of Birmingham, Ala.

The boom, once started, naturally passed up the Cumberland River to the gap in Pine Mountain, and there the Pine Mountain Coal and Iron Company, of Louisville, laid out the "city" of Pineville, now containing perhaps a thousand inhabitants, but possessing roads that would be a credit to many a larger place; water works, electric lights, a few handsome brick structures, churches, etc., all of which has been accomplished in less than two years.

Since the founding of Pineville numerous parties and corpora-. tions have been purchasing the lands to the northward, so that little of Clay, Bell, Leslie and Perry Counties remains in the hands of its native owners. Perhaps the most successful of the companies in securing a large and valuable territory is the Kentucky Coal, Iron and Development Company. It originated with three men of limited means, who began bonding the lands along the Red Bird Fork of the Kentucky River. Since then they have succeeded in enlisting English capital and are surveying and securing over 200,000 acres of land, which costs them from $2 to $10 per acre. In addition they have purchased a saw-mill and have thus secured an immediate source of income from their timber lands. So large an undertaking requires organization, and this we will endeavor to describe. The working forces, aside from the executive, can be divided into three parts. First, the buyers, a few men acquainted with the people and country, who secure options on such desirable land as is for sale; second, the legal department, which is of vital importance, for the patents under which all real estate is here held are of the most curious and fantastic shapes and are scattered two, three, and even four deep; third, the engineering or, more properly, surveying department, with which we are particularly concerned. This consists of a chief engineer, two division engineers, and about twenty survey-ors. It is the duty of the division engineers to collect all the necessary papers and to keep the surveyors supplied with them. They also have control of the men in their divisions. Com-passes (those furnished by the company and made by Gurley are supplied with a telescope and vertical circle graduated to degrees and with a vernier) and 33-foot chains are the instru-ments used. Parties consist of a compassman, two chainmen, a

flagman and an axman. Each camp consists of two parties and
a cook. After pitching tent in a new section the first thing done
is to run the meanders of the main streams and roads which pass
through the territory in question and to locate, as far as possible,
the position and general direction of the ridges and lesser streams.
At convenient intervals along these "base lines" trees are marked, being numbered in regular order from the beginning. Subse-
quently a corner of each deed or patent is tied to one of these
"bases." The surveyors' difficulties are numerous. If the seller
knows where all his corners are and his neighbors are willing
to show their corners and papers, so that interferences may be
run out, everything goes smoothly. But often papers cannot be
found, corners have disappeared and neighbors "allow" they
won't have their land run out, all of which must be overcome by
patient care and gentle persuasion.

The field work is over "sticks and stones and marrow-bones,"
over hill and valley, through briars and over cliffs, and a sorry
looking crowd comes each night to devour a steaming supper of
ham or chicken with biscuits, corn bread, canned corn, peaches
or apricots, and any vegetables or milk or butter that can be
obtained in the neighborhood, for the company is very liberal in
this direction. In the evening all there is to do is to read over
your only novel for the third time, tell stories, play cards, and
sometimes wish for civilization. But, again, it is beautiful among
the hills, and when at night the mists are slowly rising, covering
the hills with a silver veil while the moonlight scintillates on the
distant summits and illuminates the pale, passing clouds; while
afar sounds the rippling of the water over pebbles, and from hill
to hill echo and reëcho the shrill voices of night's creatures—
then you feel that amid the wilderness you are not alone; you
feel the throb of universal life, and your discontents and dis-
appointments are subdued and forgotten before the majesty of
Nature.

When all patents are run (and in running if your line strikes a
tree you simply move to the other side) and tied to the base line
a complete set of notes is sent to the headquarters camp to be
plotted, and the result is something marvelous. As a foundation
appears an old Virginia grant, commencing nobody knows where

and ending at the same place, and of course of no value, for its owners have long since failed to pay taxes on it or to claim it in any way. Next, perhaps, comes a series of long, narrow tracts following the streams and intended to cover the bottoms. Fitting on to these, or overlapping them, comes another series, reaching perhaps half way up the hills, and then three or four patents scattered at random where the owner supposed there might be some vacant land; finally, on top of all, a large "blanket" survey made during the last ten or fifteen years and covering everything. For the sum of five cents per acre and fees, you have the privilege of adding another layer, but the profit is liable to be entirely with the state.

All timber corners are located by survey on the ground and the rest of the patent is plotted according to its calls. It is not unusual to find an error of closure of 200 or 300 feet, and I remember one case where it was over half a mile. Of course the original survey had been made in a chair before a blazing fire, perhaps with a jug of "moonshine" near at hand, but so long as one or two corners were actually marked that makes no difference. The law is to draw the last line to the beginning regardless of consequences. I have known a man to find his house and the better part of his land outside the boundaries of his patents. The land was still his by possession, but the example illustrates the methods of the old surveyors. The strangest shaped patent we have met with is one that runs around itself three times, each time with a wider radius, so that, instead of covering 100 acres, it covers over 2000.

Areas are calculated by division into triangles (the scale for plots being 40 poles to the inch), and I think our results come within ½ per cent. of the actual values.

At the main camp is a quartermaster and a store tent. All supplies go there from Pineville, a distance of thirty-five miles, but such is the condition of the roads that it takes a four-mule wagon a week for each round trip. Payments for all purposes are made by check, so that an elaborate system of accounts is avoided.

The cost of the engineering department is considerable, the monthly salaries paid being about as follows: Division engineers, $110; surveyor and draughtsmen, $65 to $100 and expenses; chainmen, flagmen, etc., $1 per day, when at work, and board. Salaries for each party will average $200 per month, expenses at least $70, making, for twenty parties, $4400. The total expense of the department exceeds $6000 per month. The amount of land surveyed has averaged during the summer 1000 acres per party per month, making the cost per acre 30 cents. When the leaves fall this should be reduced to about 15 cents per acre.

Excepting at the towns of Pineville and Middlesborough, the iron and coal industry has not as yet commenced to develop. Coke of an excellent quality, comparing favorably with Pennsylvania varieties, is produced in considerable quantity. Particulars of tests, etc., may be found in the reports of the Kentucky State Geological Survey. Timber, principally poplar, is being cut in immense quantities, and one of the creeks is being provided with splash dams at a considerable cost, so that the saw-mills may be continuously supplied with logs. It is safe to say that this is destined in the near future to become one of the busiest places in the South, as the supply of hard wood cannot be exhausted in less than ten years and the amount of coal is unlimited and easy of access.   F. E. FISHER.

EMERY WHEELS.

1. Material of.
2. How made.
3. Uses of.
4. Cost.
5. Speeds.
6. Proportions of standards.

Emery is one of the hardest minerals known, ranking next to diamond in power of cutting or abrading hard substances. It is a variety of the species of corundum or sapphire of a dark reddish brown, black or gray color, and consists of nearly pure alumina and oxide of iron. It is found in large masses and much resembles fine grained iron ore, for which it has been frequently taken.

It is obtained chiefly in Asia Minor and the Island of Naxos in the Grecian Archipelago. It is also found at Chester, Mass., in a vein with magnetic iron ore, and considerable quantities have been extracted. Emery is scarcely inferior to the sapphire or ruby in hardness and was used by the ancients in cutting gems, being said to have been used for this purpose in the time of Moses. Emery is now used in the arts in a pulverized form, being obtained in various degrees of fineness by crushing and sifting in sieves having a certain number of wires to the inch. Thus what goes through a sieve having 60 wires to the inch is No. 60. The numbers range as high as 120, which is flour emery. There is a considerable difference in the abrasive power of commercial emery found in the different localities and it varies according to the composition, the state of aggregation and the purity. The better qualities of crystalline corundum are superior to emery in hardness and abrasive power and powdered sapphire to corundum. Taking the corundum of Asia Minor as 100, the emery of Kulali is 52 to 74, of Samos 73, of Nicaria 65, of Naxos 60 and that of Chester, Mass., 58. Corundum contains 92 % alumina, and emery from 60 to 78 %, with 25 to 35 % of oxide of iron and a few per cent. of silicon and water.

The methods of application are various. Lapidaries sprinkle it with water or oil on their lead wheels. Mixed with glue or other adhesive substances, it is spread in a thin layer on wood, leather, paper or cloth, or made into solid blocks or wheels, and it is in this last form, known as solid emery wheels, that it finds its widest application and greatest utility. The rapidity of abrasion depends not only on the velocity of movement, but on the size of the grains. For very heavy work, as taking the edges off castings, very coarse emery is used, while the finer grades are employed in fine grinding and surface work. We may denote the capacities for abrasion by comparing them to the cuts of files, thus:

Nos.	8 to 10	= cut of	wood rasp.
"	16 to 20	= "	rough file.
"	24 to 30	= "	middle-cut file.
"	36 to 40	= "	bastard file.
"	46 to 60	= "	second-cut file.
"	70 to 80	= "	smooth file.
"	90 to 100	= "	superfine file.
"	120	= "	flour emery.

The solid emery wheel is an American invention and the differences of different makes lie chiefly in the relative merits of the cement used to hold together the particles of emery. This cement must be strong enough to resist the tendency of the wheel to fly apart by centrifugal force due to the high speed, should not soften, warp, heat or crack under heat or pressure, or become brittle by cold. It must not form too large a percentage of the volume of the wheel, and should mix well with the emery so as to form a mixture of uniform density, for the wheel must be of uniform density and strength throughout, and perfectly' balanced. The cement should not glaze nor be of such a resistant character as to unduly heat the work in wearing down the cement to get at the emery. Therefore a wheel that lasts comparatively a very long time is not apt to be a fast and easy cutting one, and these wheels are generally the more expensive in the end.

Emery wheels are manufactured by vulcanization, by air drying and by vitrifaction. Good wheels are produced by all these processes, the successful result depending upon the ability of the manufacturer to control certain conditions. Some processes are more difficult of control than others, and the more difficult the process the greater the probabilities that poor wheels will be made. Of the various cements vulcanite was one of the earliest. Others use the gum from old leather acted on by acid, japan and linseed oil, glue, silica with calcined chloride of magnesia or "bittern water," oil and litharge, calcined chloride of zinc, celluloid and vitrified feldspar or quartzose material. Most of these require the use of high hydraulic pressure in molds, a 12-inch wheel receiving a pressure of from 150 to 200 tons. One maker puts a circle of brass wire netting in the centre of his wheels to prevent accident in case of rupture, and this same maker obtains the necessary pressure in molding by applying heat to the solidly bolted molds. The hardness of wheels is varied by the weight of mixture put into a mold of given size and in the heating the material undergoes a partial vitrifaction by which the volume tends to increase. The first thing in the manufacture of wheels is to thoroughly mix the emery and the materials which are to hold it together.

In the manufacture of vulcanite wheels, the India rubber and emery are mixed by powerful machinery, as little rubber being used as will hold the emery together. This is then rolled into sheets, cut into wheels of the desired size and form, pressed into iron molds, and vulcanized or cured by being subjected to steam heat for several hours. Previous to being vulcanized the substance is about the consistency of leather, but when vulcanized it becomes nearly as hard as cast iron and of the nature of stone throughout, but retains some elasticity, which allows the grains of emery to protrude and sharpen themselves. In the making of all wheels but the vulcanite, a very high degree of heat must be used.

The vitrification process consists in mixing emery with feldspar or other similar substances and water to form a dough. The wheels are then shaped as a potter would a piece of ware. It is then dried for some time, and after becoming perfectly dry is subjected to a very high degree of heat, 3500 degrees or thereabouts, and so continued for several days, after which a long time is required in cooling. It has been asserted that as emery contains from 25 to 30 per cent. of oxide of iron, this high heat is injurious.

Other wheels in the market are manufactured with soluble, animal, mineral and vegetable compounds, and cured by air or artificial drying. Finally the wheels are trued up with diamonds. The emery used in the manufacture of wheels in this country is our domestic emery mixed with Turkish, the domestic not being hard enough to be used alone.

In one kind of vitrified wheels, the calcining makes the wheel porous, and consequently lighter, and this property of being porous permits the wheel to receive water at its axis and deliver it at the periphery, keeping the cutting surface wet and cool without an excess of water.

Many of the cements used in the manufacture of wheels will not permit the use of water or oil on the wheels. Wheels may be molded and turned to any special shapes useful for various classes of work, and some makers produce the unusual shapes by turning up flat-faced wheels with diamond tools. Vitrified wheels may be run in oil for buffing or polishing work.

The emery wheel, made as it is in so many different shapes, has a wide range of usefulness, and may be used with great advantage and economy for cutting, grinding and finishing wrought iron, cast and chilled iron, hardened steel, slate, marble, glass, for finishing and polishing plane and cylindrical surfaces, in the manufacture of hardware, cutlery, edge tools, plows, safes, stoves, fire-arms, wagon springs, axles, skates, agricultural implements and small machinery of almost every description. They do faster and better work than a grindstone, and do work which could not be done at all on the latter with any advantage, and like a grindstone may be worn down until the size is insufficient.

When properly managed and with good workmen these wheels will be found the most effective and economical tools that can be put into a machine shop, resulting in a great saving, as they grind faster than grindstones, thus doing truer work, and do away with much filing, planing, etc. Filing, even when done by a good workman, is inaccurate, slow and expensive. For gumming or sharpening saws nothing is so simple and effective as the emery wheel, and by it a saw six feet in diameter can be thoroughly gummed and the teeth deepened to any desired extent in two hours. Not the least important function of the emery wheel is its use as a tool sharpener, and a machine for this purpose is a valuable acquisition to any machine shop. By it planer, lathe, shaper and similar tools are ground correctly, and in any machine shop whose size would warrant it a man should be employed especially to run one of these machines. The periphery of the wheel used is wedge shaped and the wheel used is generally corundum. These wheels are used wet, dust and heating of tools thus being avoided and the cutting properties of the wheels often improved.

Machines for grinding all sorts of milling tools are also made, as well as machines for grinding twist drills, there being on the market several ingenious machines for grinding twist drills to the proper angle and clearance. Flat-faced wheels are here used. Rim wheels are used in machines for grinding long knives, etc. Most makers will make any shape of face to order. "Buzzers," for grinding shoe dies, are made about 2 in. x 3 in.,

2 in. x 2½ in., 1½ in. x 1¾ in., etc. "Rolls," for grinding out the inside of journals, are of the general shape, 1½ in. x 6 in., 3½ in. x 6 in., 4 in. x 4 in., 2 in. x 4 in., etc. Wheels for grinding stove plates are 8 in. x 6 in., 8 in. x 4 in., 7 in. x 4 in., 6 in. x 5 in., 6 in. x 6 in., etc. "Cones" are made in sizes 8 in. and 7 in. x 4 in., 8 in. and 6 in. x 4 in., etc., "Pot Balls," for grinding out the inside of iron pots, 7 in. x 4 in., 6 in. x 4 in., 7 in. x 3½ in., etc. "Concave Wheels," for flat-bottomed kettles of different shapes to order, and "Skillet Wheels," for grinding out spiders of different diameters.

There is not a great deal of difference in the cost of wheels of different makes. A wheel 1½ in. x ¼ in. costs about 30 cents; a 5 in. x ½ in., about $1.40; a 16 in. x 3 in., $36.50, etc. A wheel 48 in. x 6 in. costs about $607.00, and this is about the largest wheel made.

Wheels may be made solid, with a hole in the centre for placing on a mandrel, or may be made on cast iron centres. For large wheels this method of mounting has some advantages, both as regards convenience and cost. Wheels so made should be kept in a place on the shaft or mandrel by a fixed collar on one side of the nave, and a loose collar and nut on the other, and prevented from turning on the mandrel by a spline. Wheels should never be keyed on, as this is dangerous and may throw the wheel out of true. It is absolutely necessary to the successful running of wheels that they should run true, and, hence, should be well mounted. Standards should be sufficiently heavy and well fastened down so as to be steady under the running of the wheels, for a jerking of the standard will help to break a wheel. It is troublesome and expensive to properly put up an emery wheel, and this is probably a reason for a less general use than their usefulness would seem to command, for it can be made in sizes and shapes impossible in a grindstone besides being able to resist lateral pressures which would crack a grindstone of the same shape and size. Hence its usefulness in grinding small tools, as milling tools. Many wheels are fitted with brass or lead bushings at the centre, in order that a possible high temperature may not break the wheel by expansion against a tightly fitting mandrel. In service, wheels are held between flanges screwed up by a nut, and it is a good thing to pad them with leather or something as good.

The faster an emery wheel runs the better seem to be the results obtained in grinding, but the speed is limited by practical considerations and the best results are obtained with a speed of the periphery of about 5500 feet or about a mile per minute. One maker thinks that the highest possible speed is necessary to the efficiency of a wheel and warrants a 1½ in. wheel to make from 15,000 to 24,000 revolutions per minute or 5888 to 9428 feet per minute speed of periphery, 16 in. wheels from 1550 to 2508 r.p.m., and 48 in. wheels from 525 to 846 r.p.m., or 6594 to 10,552.4 feet per minute, the greater speed being just about two miles per minute of periphery. A good thing about this high speed is that the wheels will be perfectly safe at a speed of one mile per minute, at which speed it is recommended that the wheels be run. Many consumers prefer the most durable wheel because their men are paid by the piece; and their men accept such wheels, not discovering that a great durability means a small product. The average cutting effect of a good wheel is 1.42 oz. of cast iron per minute. Wheels are largely in use cutting only .4 oz., in preference to those which could cut 5.1 oz. The workman wears himself out in pushing and loses time in hacking the wheel to sharpen it, while a quick cutting wheel practically maintains its sharpness automatically and is cheaper to use.

As the life of an emery wheel greatly depends on its being kept true it is necessary that it be regularly trued up; for, take a big man grinding a heavy casting on an emery wheel, the man presses with a good deal of force against the casting, and, if the wheels be not true, big chunks are apt to be taken off as the parts of larger diameter strike the casting and the wheel is rapidly worn away.

The best way of "trueing up" is to use what is called a diamond turning tool, made to fit into the tool stock of an ordinary lathe and having for its cutting point a small black diamond.

If the periphery of wheel be slightly heated, a vulcanite wheel may be trued up with an ordinary lathe tool, but care must be taken that too much heat is not applied, as it will injure the wheel.

The "Huntingdon Emery Wheel Dresser" is made entirely of steel, and will dress a wheel running at full speed. It is claimed that whereas it turns and shapes a wheel only that this cutter will true, shape, sharpen and remove the glaze. The tool is about 12 inches long and the head contains a series of independent sharp-toothed cutters, loosely journaled on a hardened steel pin, so that while rapidly cutting the wheel they are not perceptibly worn. Cost is $4.

Wheels should not be run on small arbors, but use the following rule: Run wheels 4 in. diameter and under on ½ in. spindles; 5 in. to 10 in. on ¾ in. spindles; 12 in. diameter on 1 in. spindle; 14 in. to 16 in. on 1¼ in. spindle; 18 in. to 20 in. on 1½ in. spindle, and 22 in. to 26 in. on 2 in. spindle. Diameter of flanges should be about ⅓ the diameter of the wheels. Length of bearings is from 32½ to 40% of the diameter of the largest wheel the machine will run. Bench space in square inches is about 13½ times the diameter of largest wheel machine will run. The machine should be fitted with good rests, and as the wheels wear away they should be moved up close to the surface of the wheel. In grinding on a wheel be careful not to bear on in any one place all the time, but keep the work constantly moving back and forth across the face of the wheel. This is important, as the wheel is worn evenly, heating is prevented, a better cutting surface is kept and a harder wheel can be used. Work should not be crowded against the wheel so as to try to force it to cut, as it will cut faster if only a moderate pressure is applied, keep cooler and last longer. A hood of cast iron about two inches thick covering almost the entire wheel is sometimes used to prevent accidents to workmen in case a wheel breaks.

While the increasing manufacture and use of improved labor-saving machinery goes on the intelligent mechanic cannot fail to see that the use of emery wheels must take an important part in reducing the cost of production to meet the sharp competition now prevailing.   J. S. HEILIG.

EDITORIAL.

THE next number of THE QUARTERLY will contain an article
by Dr. Coppée.

THE experiment of asking practical engineers their opinions
on questions that concern our graduates each year has been
a success. The next of this series will be of interest to the Mechanical Engineers.

THE replies to the series of questions in regard to the profession of engineering, found in another column, will doubtless
suggest to some of our readers, especially to those who will, next
June, embark from Lehigh's quiet harbor, several perplexing
questions.

Among the forty-five men who have nearly finished an education fitting them almost exclusively for technical pursuits, there
can hardly fail to be some who, entering Lehigh as early in life
as the average man does, find at the end of the four years that
they have mistaken their vocation. Perhaps not totally missed
the mark, but not exactly hit it. Bearing in mind the saying
about the "rolling stone," in spite of the questions coming up in
their minds as to the advisability of leaving an uncongenial•pur-
suit, they may still follow the profession of engineering, and by
diligence and perseverance achieve some success. But they will
always feel that the same energy directed in other channels
would have given greater rewards.

That oft-repeated warning against abandoning one pursuit to
follow another. Did you ever wonder, kind reader, whether it
has not prevented many lives from success? Are there not many
natural shopkeepers trying to run transits and design machines?
Are there not "born" engineers among the clergy? No doubt
each of us is cut out to fill some particular niche. And it seems
possible that half of us never find the niche. If we did, what successful men we all would be!

WHAT WE NEED.

NOW that we are to have a new Laboratory, THE QUARTERLY indulges in a few speculations. Its situation will be such as to require the formation of a second quadrangle in case new buildings are to be added to our already splendid beginning. The next building in order should be a Mechanical Hall. It is needed, and a large, fine building suitably placed would with our new Physical Laboratory beautify that spot "east of the ravine."

Then again, if we are to have the Electrical Course practical, why not light the campus and buildings by electricity, and see to it that they are well lighted? The campus would then cease to be after dark in the hands of the mob. By all means let us have a Mechanical Hall and an electric light plant for our buildings.

HIGHER EDUCATION MISAPPLIED.

PROF. GOLDWIN SMITH said the following in regard to Birchall, the young Englishman executed in Canada: "Had he, instead of being sent to college, been kept steadily at work at some useful calling, he might have gone decently, and perhaps creditably, through the world. Sending him to college, where, having no literary tastes, he was sure not to study, and where, being idle, he was also sure to be dissipated, was a mistake which sealed his doom. That no boy should be sent to college who does not show a decided inclination to study is a lesson which Birchall preached to us from a felon's grave." This may seem far-away, but the same spirit of indifference to educational advantages is in our midst.

The Library, so quiet and pervaded with incentives for application, is certainly the last place to influence the production of any but praiseworthy thoughts. But the following was produced and left in one of the alcoves, maybe by mistake, probably with the secret wish that it might find a reader: "Hooray, boys! An 8.5 in Calculus and nothing more to do for three long months! I have worked hard all the term cramming my poor head full of nonsense, and denying myself many relaxations and pleasures. Now that my labors are crowned with success, I would be less than human did I not make an effort to shut out from my mind not only the labors of the past few months, but even the results of those same labors. I believe that forgetting is not merely a negative action of the mind, that is, not merely ceasing to call to mind a fact or a formula, but that by a strong action of the will the mind can drive out facts that have found place there, not only by a gradual rusting away, but by a complete expulsion. We may leave them to droop and die away, or we may from very disgust vomit them forth, as the overloaded stomach of a glutton the unpalatable food." Maybe this represents but a single man. We hope it does. It illustrates the fact that the social custom that requires the college education of boys whose parents can afford it leads to many a dishonored life.

ORATORY AT LEHIGH.

ALTHOUGH Lehigh men at the present day do not receive ample training in oratory, they are obliged, as in the case of many like institutions, to appear upon certain occasions before the public. Say what we may, to the stranger the impressions received at one of these public events are the measure of the institution's standard.

As long as the system of honors obtains at Lehigh, no remedy can be applied to the Commencement oratory, but there is reason to believe that if the men were chosen, not as honor men, but as representative orators of the class, the occasion would be brighter. It is the contests that most concern us. *Some* of our contests have been good—

> But, och! I backward cast my e'e
> On prospects drear!
> And forward, tho' I canna see,
> I guess and fear.

One thing is certain, they could be made better. It is not prejudice to exclude a man from a contest who attempts to deal with a "wery wast" subject in a manner not at all creditable to the University, but none the less pleasant to the keen humorist. It would be best, even if it did seem a questionable proceeding—but "beggars cannot be choosers"—and as long as the supply of contestants is made up of "whipped in" candidates we must prepare for the worst.

There is a remedy, however. It is this: If we could have contests in the Freshman and Sophomore years we could then be sure of a reasonably good one in the Junior year. Every Freshman Class contains its valedictorians who would enter a contest with a good show of spirit, especially so if a prize was established. Then the Sophomore contest would have a double incentive. The hope of again winning the contest and the training for the grand finalè, the Junior Oratorical. It seems to us that '91 could not leave a more acceptable gift than to establish a fund for prizes in oratory, and confine the contestants to the two lower classes or to but one, as might be decided by the class.

WAIFS AND STRAYS.

HOW often one picks up a book and after reading a few sentences finds that the author is saying what one has thought oneself many and many a time. And yet, how much more delicately and nicely expressed. We read and recognize, and wonder why we have not that rare faculty of moulding and forming a vague, undefined idea, and in a few well-chosen words conveying our thoughts to a friend or to the reading world. The Journal of Henri-Frédéric Amiel is a volume that contains many such thoughts. Whole paragraphs seem like old friends, unchanged in feature, yet daintily clad in the garb of graceful and poetic diction. When we come across a friend like this we are taken aback for a moment. Is that courtly creature our crude thought? Modesty says no, but candor compels us to admit that even now we are cherishing the embryo of what would have developed into the same grace and beauty, if we had had the power to bring the promise to realization.

*   *   *   *

"The true secret of remaining young," says Amiel, "in spite of years, is to cherish enthusiasm in oneself by poetry, by contemplation, by charity." So much for our text. Enthusiasm is the prerogative of youth; but how is it to be maintained? Let us descend from the vague generalities of the dreamy philosopher and take a sudden plunge from charity to physical vigor, from contemplation to athletics, from poetry to — foot-ball. There is the true source of a college man's enthusiasm. Those two magic words are the well-spring of a torrent that within twenty years has deluged the old idea of education, and the ancient worthies who are trying to stem the flood are much in the position of the industrious old lady with her mop in league against the Atlantic.

These may be an extremist's views, but they are well upheld by facts. When the size of a college's freshman class is governed by a foot-ball score; when a great city is turned upside-down by a harum-scarum crowd of college boys who for three hours focus their attention on a leather ellipsoid; when a whole continent waits with eager anxiety for its morning paper with all the harrowing details, then it is time for the fossils of the forties to rouse themselves to a realization of the mighty force at work among them, and to go out and cheer on the gallant combatants, if they can articulate anything but a mathematical formula or a Greek conjugation. For cheering on the team does not mean urging them to neglect of their duties, or acknowledging the superiority of matter over mind. "*Mens sana in corpore sano*," says the popular professor; and then he pays his half-dollar, and spends a bit of his precious afternoon on the foot-ball field, among a crowd of students, learning to know them in more ways than the limited intercourse of the class-room affords; while his associate, no more learned nor scholarly than he, potters around among his old books, preferring the musty folios to the brief, exhilarating sight of sturdy youth in vigorous combat. That last sentence rather pleased the editor, and he leaned.back in his chair and gazed at it admiringly so long that the ink dried in his pen, and his thoughts followed the bad example. Then his eyes wandered to the photograph of Lehigh's foot-ball team, which occupies the position of honor on his desk, and the face of one of the most brilliant of last season's players recalled a conversation which he lately had with the original—anent the reason that impels most foot-ball men to undergo the severe course of training necessary for a position on the 'Varsity team, and the constant danger to limb — he had almost said to life—that threatens the half-back or the rusher. Is it pure love of the game? Is it a desire for the renown and honor which falls to the lot of the successful athlete? Is it merely a wish to develop his physical side? Or is it love for his Alma Mater and the wish to devote himself, body as well as mind, to increasing her repute?

The answer of the mighty man of brawn — and brain too, by the way — was that each of these elements enters in, although they are not synchronal. Young Fresh-leigh sees the foot-ball practice, and, stirred by day dreams of marvelous tackling and wonderful kicks, he casts aside all thoughts of "good times" inconsistent with his resolution, and plunges with enthusiasm into the hard course of training laid out for him. When once fairly started, however, the thoughts and indeed the possibilities of personal renown fade like a sunset, but, fascinated by the game, he plays for the game's sake. But in a year or two even this taste palls and he longs to stop, to lie aside, a passive spectator, for a season. But lo! he is bound; he cannot free himself. "The fellows would all be down on me, you know," he says, and he starts again with dogged determination and real grit. Then his patriotism, or rather his alma-matriotism, shows itself. For the sake of Lehigh's honor he works steadily at what is really distasteful to him, and, by that good old law of compensation, at the end of the season he finds himself more famous than at any time when he was working with personal aims. There might be a neat little moral drawn from this tale, but it lies beyond the editor's scope to apply this customary appendage. Let the reader—if there be any—do as he wishes.

"Lehigh is oppressively new," says the romantic mediævalist; "the smell of the varnish is still on her. She may do for the scions of the veneering family, but as for me, give me a University hoary with age and imbued with the traditions of a century or ten centuries for that matter."

"Lehigh is gloriously new," retorts the modern enthusiast; "she stands on the edge of an unconquered world, ready with the vigor of youth to plunge into the dark forests of science, and to clear the way for yet more magnificent opportunities. As for traditions, they are but stumbling blocks to progress. The less of them the better."

And both are right. Lehigh is young and she rejoices in it. But youth has its dangers as well as its possibilities. Let her not forget that the first duty of youth is respect for age. Let not our Alma Mater, in the exuberance of her first successes, be the precocious infant that develops in turn into the pert child and the uninteresting adult. Let her be modest and unassuming in her early days, and every year will bring increasing dignity and power. Touching the little matter of traditions, do not be hasty in decrying them. What are traditions? Not stumbling blocks, as young America would call them, but rather stepping stones to a higher plane of life where we can afford to get along without them. There is a certain dignity and self-respect that is to be gained by a due observance of the customs of those who have gone before; and, in a university like Lehigh, where true college spirit is wofully missing, there is nothing that could blend the men of the classes and cliques into a more harmonious whole than these self-same traditions which are sneered at as relics of barbarism. They are, however, to be used as a means, and not to be made an end, else we would degenerate into a mere body of worshipers of antiquity, without inquiring if antiquity is worth the worshiping. But as yet the traditions of Lehigh are for the most part in a condition of *non-est*-ness — pardon the barbarism, purist! —and the men here now have it in their power to obliterate those unworthy of continuance, and to establish new customs which the incoming classes will be proud to keep up. So that when the men of Ninety-one or Ninety-two bring their grandsons to be introduced to Jim, the perennial, they may find that, in addition to the good old custom of the "between-hours cigarette" in the janitor's room, will be added the new one of the Freshmen invariably relinquishing their seats to the upper classmen at that time, and that instead of one man furnishing cigarettes to the assembled multiude there will be no one without his private box of Twentieth Century Richmonds, and the cigarette sponge will be a relic of savagery. A consummation devoutly to be wished.

ORIGINAL, AND GOOD.

A PAIR OF GLOVES.

A Pair of Gloves—you say, no doubt,
A foolish thing to rhyme about.
Yet, as they lay within my hand,
And I the tapering fingers scanned,
The tiny palm, the smooth long arm,
They had for me a subtle charm,
As if, in some way, they were part
Of her, who, with consummate art,
Over her rosy finger-tips
Their slenderer fingers lightly slips,
And smiles the while—as if it graced
Those little hands to be incased
In any skin that ever grew,
On any buck, or kid, or ewe.
I do not think so! Yet should I
Say so to her, she'd quick reply—
Shorn of their rightful covering
Their daintiness would soon take wing,
Which heaven forbid! And so, my dear,
Wear out a hundred pairs a year!
So that your little hands possess
Their own accustomed loveliness.
And yet it was not of your hand
That I was thinking, understand!
But of the glove that covers it.
Until I fancied it might fit
To clothe the thought which it suggested
As in my wondering hand it rested.   w.

DIFFERENTIATION IN COLLEGE LIFE.

THE student of to-day is a conglomeration. His time is not occupied solely in intellectual pursuits. He makes them his primary end, to be sure—that is, the larger number of college men does. But the respite from curriculum requirements is spent in widely different ways. One man has musical proclivities and is fortunate enough to secure a coveted place on one or more of the University musical organizations. He employs a few hours during the week for practice, trenching, perhaps, upon the time allotted to college duties. Who shall say that his is not time well spent? Another student possesses an aptitude for athletic exercise and attains renown upon the field or diamond. He may have sacrificed his position in the class, but has by his faithful, persevering labors laid fresh laurels at the feet of his Alma Mater. Shall we justify his class-room indifference? Most certainly, because he has been training his mental powers by hours of endurance and the invention of skilful stratagems that might do honor to a Hannibal. Or the under-graduate's mind has taken a finer trend, and he sees before him visions of conquest in oratory and literary productions. · His devotion is laudable. No mean ambition stirs his soul. He is illustrating a third division, into which college life has differentiated itself. And so we might complete the catalogue that combines in distinct portions the social inclinations, the journalistic attempts, the class recognitions, and by the side of them all, as their guarantee to perfect usefulness, the religious spirit which marks the successful college man. College life is not monotonous or exclusive. It takes its absorbing individuality from this one feature.—*The Nassau Lit.*

FOR LEHIGH MEN.

THE UNIVERSITY'S FIRST FOUR YEARS.

THROUGH the kindness of Mr. Clarence Wolle, of Bethlehem, who was a member of the first class that entered Lehigh, we are enabled to give the following sketch of those early times :

The first Professor of Chemistry was Charles Wetherill. He was also at the head of the department of Physics, and was a very able and learned man.

Prof. Coppée was the first President and Wm. T. Roepper professor of Mineralogy, Geology and Blow-pipe Analysis. He was a very highly cultured man in his branch of science. Dana, the famous mineralogist, considered him his equal, and I do not doubt that he was.

Hazing? Yes, there was a great deal of trickery in those first years, and Prof. Coppée was very much annoyed by some of the things the students did. There was a very genial, jolly crowd of fellows in the University then. Miles Rock, Sam Sattler and the rest. One of the incidents which I remember was leading a mule up into the chapel hall one day.

Christmas Hall, as you know, was the first building. The chapel was on the first floor, recitations were held on the second, floor and the dormitories were on the third. The Chemical Laboratory was in the two rooms at the west end of the building. During that period the erection of Packer Hall was begun. It was finished in '68 and we moved up into the new laboratory, which occupied the place of the drawing rooms on the first floor. The laboratory was designed by Prof. Wetherill and was considered one of the finest in the country.

Mineralogy, Geology and Blow-piping were studied in a room on the second story of the Lehigh Valley telegraph office. I remember very well the first examination which was held in those subjects. It took place before quite an audience of interested people from Bethlehem. The examination was almost cruelly rigid, but so thorough were the subjects studied that not a single error was made by the whole class. I think that the students who attend Lehigh now would scarcely recognize the campus as it was twenty-five years ago. Just before an important examination, for instance, I remember a crowd of us sitting in the woods just back of Christmas Hall and discussing the situation. A few hundred yards west of the present site of Packer Hall was a rocky locality called the "Old Man's Place." A hermit made it his abode up to about 1855. Quite a stream of water ran through it and it was a favorite resort, when I was a student, for Bethlehem picnic parties.

There were five men in the first class to enter. Mr. Roepper and myself took a special course in Chemistry. No one "flunked out" of the class of '69.

The growth of the University was not very rapid, though there were about 60 or 70 students when I graduated.

HENRY S. JACOBY, C.E.

Henry S. Jacoby was born near Springtown, Pa., April 8, 1857. In 1872 he entered the preparatory department of Lehigh University and was graduated in 1877 with the degree of Civil Engineer, having received the Wilbur Scholarship at the end of the Sophomore year.

During the season of 1878 he was engaged as stadia rodman on the Lehigh District Topographical Corps of the Second Geological Survey of Pennsylvania, and in November of the same year in the United States Engineer's office at Memphis, Tenn.

After nearly a year of service at Alexandria, La., on discharge observations of the Red River and other surveys, he was retained at the office as chief draughtsman. He remained there until the spring of 1885, when all engineering improvements on the Mississippi were suspended for a year on account of the failure of Congress to pass the River and Harbor bill.

In August 1886, before the reopening of the river improvement, he was called to Lehigh University as an instructor in Civil Engineering, and remained until his election, Sept. 5, 1890, to an assistant professorship in Civil Engineering at Cornell University, in charge of Graphics and Bridge Engineering.

He is joint author with Prof. Merriman of a work on Graphic Statics, which is Part II of Merriman's series of text-books on Roofs and Bridges. He is a member of the American Association for the Advancement of Science and associate member of the American Society of Civil Engineers.

NOTES.

'74. O. M. Jenks, A.C. In charge of the Refineria de Azucer, Cardenas, Cuba.

'76. W. P. Rice, C.E. Member American Society Civil Engineers.

'83. A. E. Forstall, M.E. Jersey Street Car Works, Newark, N.J.

'84. C. O. Haines, C.E. Purchasing Agent, S. F. & W. R.R., Savannah, Ga.

'87. R. H. Phillips, C.E. Firm of Robt. A. Phillips & Son, 1425 New York Avenue, Washington, D.C.

'87. A. J. Weichardt, M.E.   At Cornell University.

'88. Wm. Bradford, C.E.   With P. R. R., at Altoona, Pa.   Married April 10, 1889.

'88. J. B. Glover, M.E.   Inventor of a new lubricator for locomotive driving and truck boxes.

'88. F. H. Knorr, A.C.   N. J. Steel Works, Newark, N. J.

'88. C. H. Miller, C.E.   Mississippi River Improvement, Greenville, Miss.

'89. P. Atkinson, M.E.   Erecting shops of Union Pacific R.R., Cheyenne, Wy.

'89. E. Campbell, B.A.   Studying for the ministry, Bethlehem, Pa.

'89. R. M. Dravo, B.S.   With Dravo & Black, agents for Spiral Tubing, Pittsburgh, Pa.

'89. J. S. Kellogg, A.C.   With Edison United Manufacturing Co., at Pottsville, Pa.

'89. A. E. Lewis, E.M.   Henderson & Lewis, Analytical and Consulting Chemists and Mining Engineers, Chattanooga, Tenn.

'89. C. H. Miller, A.C.   Assistant Chemist for Dr. F. P. Dewey, 621 F Street, N.W., Washington, D. C.

'89. C. W. Schwartz, M.E.   Assistant Millwrighting Engineer for Wm. Seller & Co., Philadelphia, Pa.

'89. F. Weihe, Instructor in Mathematics and Drawing, State Industrial College, Ames, Iowa.

'90. T. C. J. Bailey, C.E.   49 N. Ninth Street, Newark, N. J.

'90. R. S. Mercur, E.M.   L. V. Coal Co, Wilkes-Barre, Pa.

'90. R. E. Neumeyer, C.E.   Norfolk & Western Railroad, at St. Paul, Wise Co., Virginia.

'90. C. W. Platt, A.C.   Cambria Iron Co., Johnstown, Pa.

'90. S. D. Warriner, E.M.   L. V. Coal Co., Wilkes-Barre, Pa.

'90. J. R. Villalon.   Engaged in railroad work in Cuba.

'90. H. Wright.   Assistant Examiner. Patent Office, Washington, D.C.

PERIODICAL AND BOOK NOTES.

[Books, or Periodicals, which are to be reviewed or indexed, should be addressed to The Lehigh Quarterly, South Bethlehem, Pa.]

PERIODICALS FROM WHICH SUBJECTS ARE TAKEN.

FROM JANUARY 1, 1891.

TITLES.	WHERE PUBLISHED.	ABBREVIATIONS.
Abstract of Proceedings Chemical Society.	London.	Ab. Proc. Chem. Soc.
American Chemical Journal.	Baltimore.	Am. Chem. Jour.
American Engineer.	Chicago.	Am. Eng.
" Journal of Mathematics.	Charlottsville, Va.	Am. Jour. Math.
" Journal of Science.	New Haven, Ct.	Am. Jour. Sci.
" Machinist.	New York	Am. Mach.
" Manufacturer and Iron World.	Pittsburg, Pa.	Am. Mfg. and I. W.

Analyst, The	London.	The Analyst.
Annaler der Physik und Chemie.	Leipzig.	An. der Ph. und Ch.
Annales de Chemie et de Physique	Paris.	An. de Ch. et de Ph.
" des Mines.	Paris.	An. des Mines.
" des Ponts et Chaussies	Paris.	An. des Ponts, et Ch's.
Astronomical Journal.	Boston.	Astron. Jour.
American Architect.	Boston.	Am. Arch.
Berg und Hüttenmännisches Jahrbuch.		Berg und Hüt. J.
" " " Zeitüng	Leipzig.	Berg und Hüt. Z.
Bulletin de la Society Chemique de Paris.	Paris.	Bull. Soc. Chem.
" " " " Industrielle de Mulhouse.	Paris.	Bull. Soc. Ind.
" of the Iron and Steel Association.	Philadelphia.	Bull. I. and St'l. Ass.
Chemical News.	London.	Chem. News.
Der Civilingenieur.	Leipzig.	Der Civ.
Dingler's Polytechnisches Journal.	Stuttgart, Ger.	D. Poly. Jour.
Engineering.	London.	Eng.
Engineering and Building Record.	New York.	Eng. Build. Rec.
" " Mining Journal.	New York.	Eng. Min. Jour.
" News.	New York.	Eng. News.
Electrical World.	New York.	Elec. World.
Electrician.	London.	Elec'n.
Iron.	London.	Iron.
Iron Age.	New York.	I. Age.
Journal of Analytical and Applied Chemistry.	Easton, Pa.	Jour. Anal. and Ap. Chem.
" " Gas Lighting.	London.	Jour. Gas Light.
Journal of the Chemical Society.	London.	Jour. Chem. Soc.
" " the Franklin Institute.	Philadelphia.	Jour. Frank. Inst.
" " the Society of Chemical Industry.	London.	Soc. Chem. Ind.
La Lumierie Electrique.	Paris.	La Lum. Elec.
Leibig's Annaler der Chemic.	Leipzig.	Leib. An. der Chem.
Memoirs de la Societe' des Ingenieurs Civils.	Paris.	Mem. Soc. Ing. Civ.
Oesterreichesche Zeitschrift für Berg un Hüttenwesen.	Wien.	Oes. Zeit. Berg un Hüt.
Proc. Eng. Club of Philadelphia.	Philadelphia.	Proc. Eng. C. of Phil.
Railroad and Engineering Journal.	New York.	R. R. Eng Jour.
Railroad Gazette.	New York.	R. R. Gazette.
Revue Universelle des Mines.	Paris.	Rev. Uni. Mines.
Science.	New York.	Science.
Scientific American.	New York.	Sci. Amer.
" " Supplement.	New York.	Sci. Amer. Sup.
Trans. Am. Soc. Civil Engineers.	New York.	Trans. Am. Soc. Civ. Eng.
Zeitschrift des Vereins Deutsch Ingeneure.	Berlin, W.	Zeit. Deut. Ing.
" für das Berg Hütten und Salinen Wesen.	Berlin.	Zeit. Berg Hüt S. Wesen.

PERIODICAL AND BOOK NOTES. 61

INDEX TO SUBJECTS FROM TECHNICAL PERIODICAL LITERATURE.

Aurora Problem, A Solution of. Am. Jour. Sci., Feb.
Artillery, Modern French. Eng. 51: 3, 30, 78, 91.
Architecture, Austrian. Am. Arch.: 3, 19, 35, 51.
Architecture, Ancient, For Students. Am. Arch.: 7, 42.
Apartment Houses. Am. Arch.: 37, 20.
Alimentation as a Therapeutic Measure. Sci. Am., Sup. 12: 509.
Ammonia, On some Constants of. Jour. Frank. Inst., 81: 71.
Analysis of Cupric Bromide and the Atomic Weight of Copper. Chem. News, 63: 20, 34.
Angle, the Economical (Structural). Sci. Am. Sup., 31: 12541.
Aluminum and Other Metals, Mfg. of. Sci. Am. Sup., 31: 12550.
Albumen in Urine, Estimation of. The Analyst, 41, 7.
Air Pump Governor, Improved. Sci. Am. 64: 35.
Cyanides and Ammonia, Artificial Production of. Sci. Am. 64: 40.
Aluminum, Fabrication de le, Procédé Employé par la Compagnie de Reduction de Pittsbourg. La Lum. Elec. 29.
Arch Joints, Line of Pres. in. Der Civ. 564.

Building Materials, Cements, Useful Stones. Chem. Tech. Rep.
Bridges (Railway), Some Recent Construction of. Sci. Am. Sup., 31: 12543.
Butter, On the Composition of. The Analyst, 41: 1.
Butter, Cocoanut. Sci. Am., 64: 20.
Bridges, Live Load and Weights of. Eng. News, 28.
Bridges, Proper Rolling Load for. Eng. News, 37.
Brick, Permeability of. Eng. News, 17.
Brooklyn Bridge, Expert Report on. Eng. News, 85; Eng. Min. Jour, 51: 84.
Brick Pavements. Eng. Record, 103.
Bridge, The Forth. Zeit. Deut. Ing., 8.
Boilers, Experiments with Red Hot Steam. Am. Mfg. & I. W., 48: 34.
Basic Bessemer Process, Weddings. 51: 111.
Basic Steel Patents. Am. Chem. Jour., 25: 4, 20.

Catalpa, The. Sci. Am. Sup., 31: 12537.
Compressed Air for Power Distribution. Sci. Am. Sup., 12519.
Cement Tester, Improved. Sci. Am. Sup., 31: 12326.
Coal Fields of Alabama. Sci. Am. Sup., 31: 12530.
Cotton Seed Oil, New Use of. Sci. Am., 64: 20.
Cyclones and Areas of High Pressure. Science, 38.
Cork Industry of Spain. Science, 20.
Corinth Canal. Eng. News, 56.
Cement Laboratory, St. Louis Iron Works. Eng. News, 2.
Copper Extraction Process, Hunt & Douglass. Berg und Hut. Z.
Connecting Rods and Crank Pins, Class "H" Engine, C. B. & Q. R. R. R. R. Gaz., 23: 39.
Copper Smelting, Basic Linings in. Eng. 51: 76.

62   PERIODICAL AND BOOK NOTES.

Crane, Jib, Application of Power to. Amer. Mach., 14: 4: 1.
Chemistry, New Basis for. Eng. Min. Jour., 51: 110.
Conductors, Economy in (Elec.). Elec. W., 17: 22.

Detecting Presence of Thäzole. Liebig's An. der Chem.
Determination of Very Small Quantities of Cast Iron and Aluminum in Cast Iron and Steel. Chem. News, 63: 10.
Drainage System, Chicago (Report). Eng. News, 87.
Dynamos and Motors, Design of. Elec. W., 17: 18.

Electricity in Mining. Eng. Min. Jour., 51: 58.
Electric Motor, Small, For Amateurs. Sci. Am. Sup., 12510.
Electric Power Transmission in Mining. Sci. Am. Sup., 12511.
Electromotive Force of Cells, Variations of. Chem. News., 63: 2.
Entomology, Outlook for Applied. Sci. Am. Sup., 31: 12538.
Exhibition, Chicago International. Sci. Am. Sup., 12514.
Electric Welding. Sci. Am. Sup., 31: 12546.
Electro-Magnet, The. Sci. Am. Sup., 31: 12547, 12522.
Educational Progress in Japan. Science., 23
Électricité, Les Progress de la, en 1890. La Lum. Elec., 8.
Électricité, Revue des Travaux récents en. La Lum. Elec., 40.
Electric Motor for Passenger R. R. Eng. News., 61.
Electro-Magnetic Radiation, Measurement of. Elec'n., 26: 302.
Electric Arc, Alternating, Between a Ball and a Point. Am. Jour. Science., Jan.
Electricity, Dangers in Connection With. Am. Arch., 8.
Electric Wiring. Am. Arch., 44.
Electrical Undulations, Resumé of. Exp. Elec. W., 17: 25.
Electro-Magnetic Radiation, Measurement of. Elec'n., 26: 302.
Engines, New Hot Air. D. Poly. Jour., 2.
Engine, Stationary, Practice in Am. Eng., 51: 1.

Fire Extinguisher, Godfrey's. Sci. Am. Sup., 12543.
Fire Resisting Construction. Eng. Rec.
Fatty Bodies in Vegetable Organisms. Am. Chem. Jour., 13: 13.

Gold and Silver, The Cyanide Process of Extracting. Eng. Min. Jour., 51: 59, 86.
Gas System, The Pintsch. Sci. Am. Sup., 12508.
Girder, The Continuous. Jour. Frank. Inst., 81: 30.
Gaseous Illuminants. Chem. News., 63: 3, 15, 32.
Guns, The Lebel and Mannlicher. Sci. Am. Sup., 12505.
Geological Soc. of America. Sci. Am., 64: 16.
Ginseng, The. Sci. Am., 64: 19.
Gas, The Chemistry of Illuminating. Jour. Gas Light., 57: 16.
Gas Coals of the U. S. Jour. Gas Light., 57: 22, 67.
Granulator, Buchanan's. Eng. Min. Jour., 51: 87.

Hydrazoic Acid, a New Gas. Sci. Am. Sup., 12533.
Healthful Homes. Sci. Am., 64: 33.
Hints to be Heeded. Sci. Am., 64: 36.

Infection, Mechanism of. Sci. Am. Sup., 31: 12539.
Induction and its Proposed Unit. Elec'n, 26: 267, 305.

Koch's Cure, The Medical Press on. Science, 43.

Lead Ores, The Potassium Cyanide, Assay of. Chem. News, 63: 30.
Locomotives as Studied by Photography. Sci. Am. Sup., 12532.
Locomotives, Comparative Study of Simple and Compound. R. R. Gaz., 23: 20.
Locomotives, Grate Surface, etc. Am. Mach., 14: 2: 1.

Markets, Metals, Ores, Stocks, and Implements. Eng. & Min. Jour., 51: 1.
Maple Molasses, Improved Process for Manufacture of. Sci. Am. Sup., 31: 12546.
Meteorite, A New Kansas. Science, 3.
Mineral Waters of Yellowstone Park. Science, 36.
Mecaniques de l'Électricité. La Lum. Elec., 19.
Moteur à Petrole Daimler. La Lum. Elec., 36.
Mechanical Drawing, The Essentials of. R. R. & Eng. Jour., 45: 37.
Mining, The Profits of. Eng. Min. Jour., 51: 110.
Men of Millions, List of. Am. Chem. Jour., 25: 18.

Nitrogen, Atmospheric, Acquisition of by Planets. Am. Chem. Jour., 13: 42.
Nickel Mines, The Sudbury, of Canada. Am. Chem. Jour., 25.

Open Hearth, Practical German Basic. Iron Age.
Ore Dock. Eng. Min. Jour., 51: 62, 88, 116.
Open Hearth Steel Process, Kupelweiser. Eng. Min. Jour., 51: 86.

Plants, Dissemination of. Sci. Am. Sup., 31: 12535.
Powder, Smokeless. Sci. Am., 64: 21.
Pipe, Covering Cast-iron Cooled Water. Eng. News, 2.
Power, Measurement of. Amer. Mach., 14: 1: 1, 3: 3.

Railway, The Metropolitan, of Paris. Sci. Am. Sup., 12504.
Reservoir, Storage and Distributing at Buffalo. Eng. News, 26.
Riveting Machines, New. D. Poly. Jour., 13.
Rope Driving. Am. Mach., 14: 3: 3.
Ropes, Long Splice for. Sci. Am., 64: 40.
Ropes, Wire. Eng. News, 50.
Russell Process vs. the Amalgamation. Eng. Min. Jour., 51: 59.
Sugar Items, New. Sci. Am., 64: 24.
Securité de l'éclairage Électrique. La Lum. Elec., 14.
Sewerage System of W. Troy, N. Y. Eng. News, 4.

Sewers. Eng. News, 4.
Steam and Water Power, Cost of. Eng. News, 75.
Steel Tubes, Spirally Welded. Iron, 37 : 30.
Screw, Efficiency of Power. Iron Age, 47 : 7.
Steel, Sulphur in Bessemer. Iron Age, 47 : 148.
Safe Building. Am. Arch., 39.
Structures, Stress in. Am. Mach., 14: 4: 3.
Sugar Series, Synthetical Experiments. Am. Chem. Jour., 13; 63.
Steel, Mild and Soft. Am. Chem. Jour., 25 : 11.

Thermometer with Electric Transmission. Sci. Am. Sup., 31 : 12549.
Tube, New Flexible. Sci. Am. Sup., 31 : 12526.
Timber, Preservation of. Sci. Am., 64 : 5.
Télégraphie, La. La Lum. Elec., 10.
Towage in Canals. Eng. News., 52.
Tunnel, The Zig-zag, N. Y., O. & W. R. R. Eng. News., 26.
Testing Machine, 1200 Tons, at Phœnixville, Pa. Eng. News, 42.
Tin in Central Texas. Eng. Min. Jour., 51 : 117.
Tunneling, New Method. Eng. Rec., 76.

Ventilation Scheme for the Patent Cupel at the Prosper Mine. Zeit. fur das Berg Hüt. S., p. 347.
Viaduct, The Brooklyn. Sci. Am., 64 : 5.
Vulcanite, Physical Properties of. Am. Jour. Sci., Jan.
Ventilating Fan, The Murphy "Champion." Eng. Min. Jour., 51 : 67.

Water Pipes, Wooden. Sci. Am., 64 : 23.
Water Works at Gouverneur, N. Y. Eng. News., 89.
Water Supply of Genoa, Italy. Eng. Rec., 122.
Water Supply, Eng. Rec., 126.
Water Works, Rochester. Eng. Rec., 109.

Zinc, Determination of, in Iron Ores. Chem. News., 63 : 25.
Zinc Powder, Valuation of. Chem. News, 63 : 12.

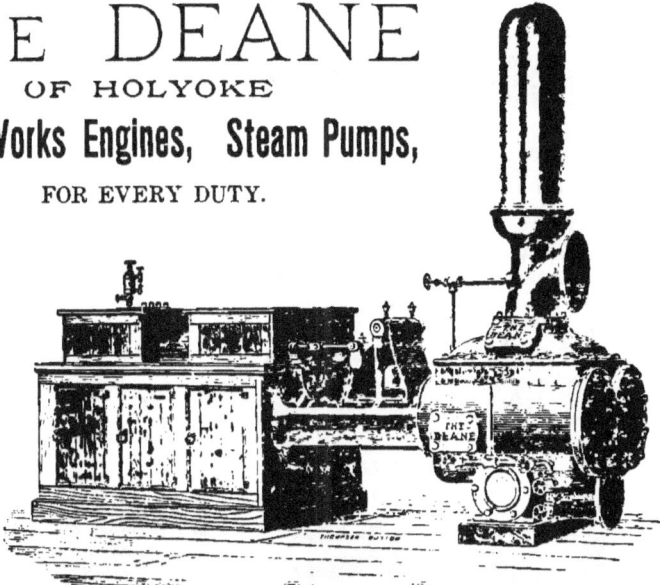

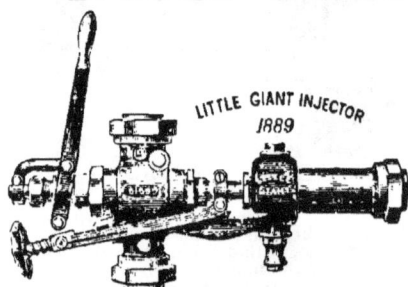